LIFE WORLD LIBRARY

TURKEY

by Desmond Stewart

and The Editors of LIFE

TIME INCORPORATED   NEW YORK

COVER: In the amber haze
of the setting sun,
the mosques and minarets
of Istanbul rise
behind the bustling water traffic
of the Golden Horn.

ABOUT THE WRITER

Desmond Stewart, author of the interpretive text for this volume in the LIFE World Library, is a British writer with wide experience in the Middle East. After completing graduate studies at Oxford in 1948, he taught literature in Iraq and Lebanon from 1948 to 1958 and traveled widely in Turkey as well as in the Arab world. A poet and a translator of Arab literature, Mr. Stewart has contributed articles on Middle Eastern affairs to a number of British and American publications. In 1964 the British Broadcasting Corporation broadcast two programs in which he gave a detailed exploration of Arab culture in the postwar years. He is also the author of several novels with Middle Eastern backgrounds, including *Stranger in Eden* and *The Men of Friday,* and of *The Arab World,* another volume in the LIFE World Library. Mr. Stewart, who spends most of each year in the Middle East, is at present engaged on a trilogy entitled *The Sequence of Roles,* the first volume of which, *The Round Mosaic,* was published in 1965.

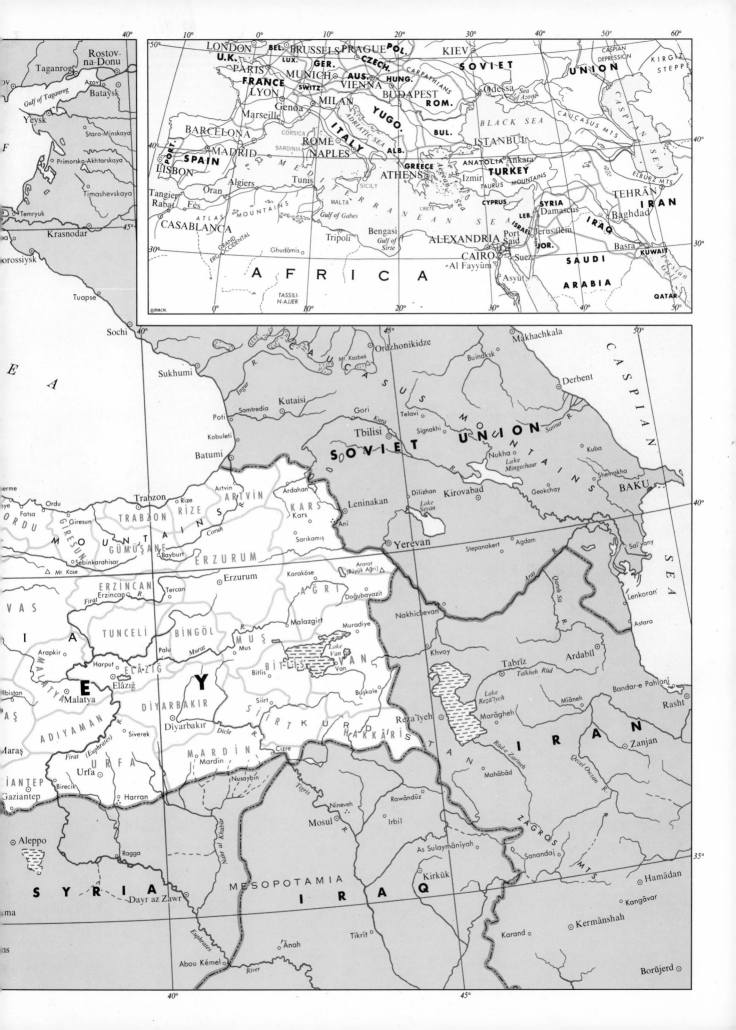

LIFE WORLD LIBRARY

TURKEY

TIME LIFE BOOKS

Contents

TIME-LIFE BOOKS

EDITOR
Norman P. Ross
EXECUTIVE EDITOR
Maitland A. Edey
TEXT DIRECTOR   ART DIRECTOR
William Jay Gold   Edward A. Hamilton
CHIEF OF RESEARCH
Beatrice T. Dobie
Assistant Text Director: Jerry Korn
Assistant Art Director: Arnold Holeywell
Assistant Chief of Research: Monica O. Horne

•

PUBLISHER
Rhett Austell
General Manager: Joseph C. Hazen Jr.
Business Manager: John D. McSweeney
Circulation Manager: Joan D. Manley

LIFE MAGAZINE

EDITOR: Edward K. Thompson
MANAGING EDITOR: George P. Hunt
PUBLISHER: Jerome S. Hardy

LIFE WORLD LIBRARY

SERIES EDITOR: Oliver E. Allen
Editorial Staff for *Turkey:*
Assistant Editor: Jay Brennan
Designer: Ben Schultz
Chief Researcher: Grace Brynolson
Researchers: Irene Ertugrul, Evelyn Hauptman, Donald Newton, Madeleine Richards, Ava Weekes, Ellen Youngblood

EDITORIAL PRODUCTION
Color Director: Robert L. Young
Copy Staff: Marian Gordon Goldman, Patricia Miller, Dolores A. Littles
Picture Researchers: Margaret K. Goldsmith, Joan T. Lynch
Art Assistants: Douglas B. Graham, John M. Woods

The text for the chapters of this book was written by Desmond Stewart; the picture essays were written by George Constable. Many of the photographs were taken by Farrell Grehan. Valuable help was provided by the following individuals and departments of Time Inc.: Ralph Morse, LIFE staff photographer; Doris O'Neil, Chief, LIFE Picture Library; Content Peckham, Chief, Bureau of Editorial Reference; and Richard M. Clurman, Chief, TIME-LIFE News Service.

Introduction

In February 1952 an event took place in a modest brownstone building in Ankara that, in a very real sense, represented the culmination of nine centuries of Turkish history. On that occasion the Grand National Assembly of Turkey, in a unanimous vote, accepted an invitation to membership in the North Atlantic Treaty Organization.

The historic impulse that led to this event really began in the 11th Century, with the westward movement from Central Asia of the Seljuk Turks—followed over the next several centuries by thousands of their fellow Turks—into the peninsula of Asia Minor. The vote of the Turkish assembly also fulfilled the vision of one of the most extraordinary men of our times—Kemal Atatürk. In Turkey's darkest hours following World War I, Atatürk by sheer will power took the Turkish nation by the scruff of its neck, shook it loose from the stifling ties of its past, and turned it resolutely to the West and to the future.

Modern Turkey, a vigorous, up-and-coming nation of 31 million people, provides a sharp contrast with the Turkey of the past. The new nation must not only compete with the greatness of the Ottoman Empire, which at its height controlled large segments of the world, but must seek to erase the image of the empire in its period of decline after 1683.

Through centuries of wars and diplomatic intrigues the dominating "fact of life" for all Turks has been the unrelenting hostility of Russia. Since the 17th Century the Turks have fought at least a dozen wars with Russia. In joining NATO Turkey became assured—for the first time in its history—that in its defense against the Soviets it will in the future have the most powerful nations of the West as its allies. Similarly, the other NATO members found in Turkey a resolute partner, an eastern anchor to NATO, capable of holding a Soviet flanking move through the Middle East. No matter what steps the Turks may take to normalize their relations with the U.S.S.R., no one need fear that the Turks will ever let down their guard against their traditional enemy.

Since the early 1920s the new Turkey created by Kemal Atatürk has taken long strides into the modern era. Progress has by no means been even. There have been setbacks and disappointments. Yet the ancient plains, rimmed by majestic mountains facing the sea, show everywhere the signs of progress: highways, schools, modern buildings, the beginnings of industrialization. The symbol of this modern Turkey is the glistening city of Ankara, grown since Atatürk's time from a town of less than 30,000 people to a city of almost a million. Ankara's roots, as Atatürk wished, lie in the dark brown soil of Anatolia.

Democracy in Turkey, which was given its form by Atatürk, achieved substance in 1950 when it met the only true test—a peaceful change in power through the free vote. Some have been concerned that the roots of Turkish democracy are shallow. I believe, however, that the Turkish people, who suffered so much in winning their freedom from autocratic rule, will never again surrender it. Turkey has recently established an association with the European Common Market. In daily participation in the NATO Council and in the Organization for Economic Cooperation and Development, Turkey plays an increasingly important role among the nations of the West—to which it is now inextricably joined.

Mr. Desmond Stewart has made a valuable contribution to the understanding of modern Turkey by his deep insight into Turkey's rich past and its challenging present. He has caught the spirit and meaning of the vigorous stream of life of this gifted people. Even though there are perhaps a few value judgments with which some readers, including myself, may differ somewhat, judgments on so complex a subject necessarily are difficult and I admire his courage in making them.

—GEORGE C. MCGHEE
former U.S. Ambassador to Turkey

1

Bridge between Continents

SOME countries are fixed termini. Others are wayside halts. Some are junctions. A few are stations closed to traffic. The country known as Turkey is a bridge linking Europe to Asia—a bridge of the ancient type, used not only as a means of transport but also as a base on which to build homes.

Turkey's western bridgehead, standing foursquare at the southeastern extremity of Europe, is the former capital of two empires, the Byzantine and then the Ottoman. Long known as Constantinople, in memory of its founder, the Christian Emperor Constantine, the city was also for many centuries known to the Turks as Istanbul, and it officially received that title in 1930. Constantinople was for

16 centuries a major factor in the politics of the world. Today no longer a capital, Istanbul shows its demotion in a certain shabbiness that contrasts with its cosmopolitan clash of cultures. Its twisting, cobbled streets tangle over seven hills. The city was not meant for automobiles, yet it is full of them. It is noisy, restless and confusing. Only its setting is unimpaired. The city rests on the Bosporus, the narrow stretch of water that separates Europe and Asia. Istanbul is built where a scimitar of water known as the Golden Horn cuts into the European shore, providing a magnificent anchorage for ships. The original capital of both the Byzantines and the Ottomans lay on the western side of the Golden

Horn, but the modern city has expanded across the Horn to the eastern side. It now includes Beyoğlu, or Pera, once a base for European merchants. It also includes several municipalities on the Asian shore, to which ferryboats make frequent runs.

A ferryboat journey from Europe to Asia lasts about 20 minutes or less. As the bells clang, as little glasses of tea are brought to the seated passengers, as the boat moves into mid-Bosporus and the skyline of the old city with its many vast mosques recedes, a contrast of types can be seen. The *efendi* —the cultivated, urban Turk—sits in his raincoat perusing his newspaper; his uncorseted wife reads a novel translated from French; his children in neat suits sit by demurely. In the second class sit peasants. Their clothes are shabby, and at first sight their faces seem grim and humorless. Yet a word spoken, a question asked, in either class, and the dourness dissolves into a willingness to help that would be rare anywhere. To the stranger comes the clink of the spoon in a proffered tea glass as sudden friends offer him a cordiality which is not the less for being inarticulate. The dourness, one suddenly realizes, exists only on the surface and hides inner kindness.

Dourness concealing gentleness is a feature of the harsh mainland which begins as the ferry touches the Asiatic shore. The name of the mainland mass which stretches to the frontiers of Russia and Iran far to the east is Anatolia, or in Turkish, *Anadolu*, a word derived from Greek and meaning, simply, "the east." In the south the Anatolian plateau overlooks the shimmering depression of Iraq, whose two major rivers—the Tigris and the Euphrates— stem from Turkey's hills. On the eastern frontier, where rears the elephantine lump of Mount Ararat, the Anatolian bridge merges imperceptibly with the great approach roads to Central Asia. Yet the interchanges between East and West which mark the

Bosporus or the busy markets of the old city are absent. The people of the rugged mountains hardly seem en route anywhere; their poverty, their dung fires, their mountain bigotry bind them to an East that extends through Iran and Afghanistan to the Indus valley and beyond.

Yet even in Turkey's most isolated villages— clusters of mud-built houses set among barren hills, a day's ride from the nearest hard-surfaced road— villagers dream of moving west, and in a constant trickle they put their dreams to the test. Istanbul and the bigger cities of Anatolia are constantly swelling in size as those without work or hope of advancement join relatives who had moved to the cities before them.

The dream of westward movement is by no means new; despite Alexander the Great, who took his legions from Greece across Anatolia and into India in a great surge eastward in the Fourth Century B.C., the movement of history in the last 8,000 years has largely been from the east to the west—and Anatolia has played a major role in that movement. To it have come successive waves of peoples from deep in Central Asia, some to settle and some to pass on into the Balkans and beyond.

But if Anatolia has served as a bridge, it has also erected geographic barriers to movement which have made it difficult to cross, at least until modern times. It provides the kind of landscape which molds and modifies those who move through it, not only those who live in its midst all the time. Continental in size, although in shape a squat peninsula, the country has distinct and varied regions. The silt-bearing rivers of the fertile valleys of western Anatolia flow into an Aegean where one mountainous island after another fills a magic horizon. Once this fretted coastline is left, however, the country becomes a stern land from which all Mediterranean

---

REJECTING THE ARABIC SCRIPT

The Turks wrote in Arabic script until Kemal Atatürk forced a change to a Latin alphabet in 1928. Arabic writing had never suited Turkish, as the examples shown here demonstrate. Turkish has eight vowels, but the Arabic alphabet has letters for only three. Moreover, some Arabic consonant symbols can be pronounced in various ways in Turkish: the symbol *"kef"* can denote a *"g"* or a *"k"* sound. Thus the letters *"kef," "vav," "ri"* (Arabic is read from right to left) could be pronounced either as *"gör,"* meaning "see," or as *"kör,"* meaning "blind." Since Arabic lacks letters for the sounds *"e"* and *"ü,"* the word intended by the characters *"kef"* and *"lam,"* which denotes an *"l"* sound, could be *"gel,"* meaning "come," *"gül,"* "rose," *"kel,"* "bald."

LAM KEF

RI VAV KEF

softness vanishes like mist from a lawn. Central Anatolia is an upland plateau with rolling plains and heavy seasonal rainfall. The fruit of the rain is a series of vast lakes. Surrounding Burdur, a saline lake empty of fish, the hills are stale and ocherous; around Eğridir, a fresh lake, the hills are verdant. If these lakes are the sumps for deluging rainfall, the surrounding prairies, sticky mud seas when the rain is falling, change to dust bowls when all moisture dries up in the almost Arab sun of July and August.

Summers are dry in the uplands. But in one Turkish region—the Cukurova valley south of the Taurus Mountains which wall central Anatolia off from the Mediterranean—the summers are as humid as are those of the Egyptian delta. Like the delta, this steamy flatland centered on the great city of Adana is laid out in cotton fields, with here and there a medieval castle rising on some eccentric crag.

Eccentricity is almost the rule in Anatolia. Just when the visitor has become used to one particular rhythm, something completely bizarre strikes him. At Pamukkale, whose name means "cotton castle," calcium streams have solidified into frozen white confectionery; cloth placed in local water stiffens quickly. Farther east, in Cappadocia (Urgüp), volcanic debris scattered by some prehistoric upheaval has been eroded into thousands of easily worked chimneys used in the past as hermits' cells and today as troglodytes' homes. Located in central Anatolia, Cappadocia marks the point where the plateau begins to tilt upward. The tilt is toward the east, where Erzurum stands 6,400 feet above sea level as the military guardpost of eastern Turkey. A grim city with a severe climate, Erzurum is scarcely larger than many other towns which dot these eastern highlands. Seen from the air, Sıvas, Bitlis, Muş and Erzurum itself all mark minuscule pockets of fertility and workable earth in savage, rolling hills

through which no road seems to wind. Only in the valleys are there trees. Yet if, instead of flying eastward toward the frontier with the U.S.S.R. and Iran, the plane heads north toward the sea, the mountains suddenly change color. Behind Trabzon, near the ridge where the Greek mercenaries of Xenophon 23 centuries ago first beheld the Black Sea after their trek through Asia—and in their relief shouted, "The sea! The sea!"—the foothills are covered with the green of hazel groves.

So great is the variety in the Turkish landscape that it has often been said that nearly every European zone can find its counterpart in Anatolia. Turkey shows a similar variety in its people. The term "Turks" is used officially for all citizens, but colloquially it is employed only to describe the Moslems, who constitute 98 per cent of the population. Even when restricted solely to the Moslems, the term encompasses a wide gamut of human types. Except for tiny colonies descended from African servants (there is one such by the waterfalls of Manavgat in the south), most Turks are pale-skinned. The upland Turks seem a blend of a squat, stocky type and something more Eastern, noticeable in the cut of the eye and the cast of the cheekbone—a reminder that the first people to be known as Turks originated within call of China and Korea. In the valleys near the sea, where many citizens descend from Greeks who embraced Islam, the Turks tend to be slighter, more European.

The Kurds, who number between 1.5 and 2.5 million people, are Anatolia's largest minority. They live in the mountainous regions of eastern and southern Anatolia, are often fair and speak a language that is closely akin to Persian. They are part of a submerged nation straddling the frontiers of Turkey, Syria, Iran and Iraq. In Iraq they have been waging an explicit war for national autonomy. In Turkey,

---

ACCEPTING A NEW ALPHABET

The modified Latin alphabet that was adopted in 1928, and that is used for Turkish words in this book, contains one new letter, "ı," known as the "undotted i," and several letters that use diacritical marks as an aid to pronunciation. The character "ı" represents a short consonant sound similar to the "u" in "radium" —as in *fırın* (pronounced *furun*), meaning "oven." The regular "i" is like the English "i" in "pit," as in *bir*, which means "one." The "ç," found in *çatal*, meaning "fork," is pronounced like the English "ch." The "ş," pronounced like "sh," is found in *şapka*, the word for "hat." The "ğ" is something like the "y" in "yes," as in *boğaz*, meaning "throat," and is sometimes used to lengthen a preceding vowel. The "ö" is like the "eu" in the French word *"deux,"* and the "ü" is much like the German "ü" in *Führer*. An example is the word *"ünsiyet,"* which means "familiarity."

there has been less manifestation of discontent since the Kurds launched a large-scale rebellion in 1925 and other revolts in 1930 and 1937.

This variety of face and figure, this evidence of history's slow amalgamation, is set among Eastern motifs. The skylines of Turkish cities are marked by domes and minarets. The domes are a derivation from the cupolas of Byzantium; the pencil-thin minarets are a specifically Turkish evolution from the towers or platforms which the first Moslems—those of Arab lands—used for the call to prayer. The Eastern motifs are not only physical. In the villages the Eastern dominance of male over female still persists. In heavy rain women trudge out to work in the fields, their babies on their backs; in the coffeehouses the men patiently play backgammon, waiting for the women to return to cook their food.

YET the people in this background, behaving in this way, are dressed in Western clothes— or, let us say, they wear clothes that were Western and modern 40 years ago. The effect is drab. A Turkish crowd resembles, in its gray cloth caps, its shabbily cut trousers and jackets, a throng of unemployed steelworkers from the years of the Depression, not the "parterre of tulips" evoked in a famous description of 18th Century Turkish men by the British traveler Lady Mary Wortley Montagu. But just as the Western clothes conceal a largely Eastern way of life, so the dearth of smiles conceals good spirits. It is a feature of the Turks to look depressed when in fact they are feeling either happy or content.

Contrast and paradox have always been features of Turkish daily life. These contrasts have not diminished but, rather, have increased since the collapse of the Ottoman Empire after World War I was followed by the installation of a new regime headed by the man known as Atatürk, who strove to make of Turkey a Western nation, one proudly aware of the glories of its Turkish rather than its Ottoman roots. One of Atatürk's most far-reaching acts was to order that Turkish henceforth be written in Latin rather than Arabic script, despite the fact that many Turkish words are Arabic in derivation. Consequently, a modern Turkish schoolboy writes in his *defter* (the Arabic noun for "exercise book") from left to right, as do children in the West. His grandfather's

gravestone bears an inscription in Arabic script reading from right to left, which the boy and everyone else under 45 cannot read. As well as changing the letters, Atatürk often insisted on changing the words of Turkish. As a result the boy's teacher has changed in a generation from being called *muallim* (the word derived from Arabic) to *öğretmen* (the "purer" Turkish word). When the boy grows up and makes a reference to a *defter* he may be met with incomprehension; a "pure" Turkish word may have been found for that, too.

WHEN the boy does reach manhood he will almost certainly marry. Turkish bachelors are rare. His marriage, in Western clothes before a civil authority, will, if he lives in a big city, perhaps be followed by slightly out-of-date Western dancing—the Turks being conservative even in their modernism. His grandmother, who was married before the passage of the Civil Code of 1926, knew a different ceremony. She hid behind the door while her bridegroom made his marriage pledges before an all-male gathering presided over by an imam, or Moslem clergyman. The girl answered from her place of concealment.

Yet old ways persist. In the remoter Anatolian villages the hour of the day is reckoned not by clocks, which few villagers possess, but by the times appointed for the daily prayers of Islam. Nor are dates reckoned exactly. A Turkish writer born in a village has told how neither his mother nor his father could tell him the exact year he was born. Each fumbled for some guiding event: a flood in which some children had been drowned, or the time when the boy's father finished his military service, an event which itself could be dated only by reference to the year a village poplar was struck by lightning.

Although Atatürk's revolution was in some ways hostile to religion, more Turks now make the pilgrimage to Mecca than did so when the railway to Arabia's holy places was the proudest achievement of Ottoman Turkey. As many mosques as schools are estimated to have been built in the period between 1950 and 1960.

Long before Turkey put on its modern overcoat, observers had been struck by the union of opposites in the Turkish character. "The national character of the Turks," wrote Thomas Thornton, a British merchant, in 1807, "is a composition of contradictory qualities. We find them brave and pusillanimous; gentle and ferocious; resolute and inconstant; active and indolent; passing from devotion to obscenity, from the rigor of morality to the grossness of sense; at once delicate and coarse, fastidiously abstemious and indiscriminately indulgent." So that according to this contemporary of Lord Byron, writing long before modernization, the Turks were people interestingly poised between extremes.

They remain so. An often-repeated story tells of a young British journalist who shared a compartment with some Turkish conscripts on a train trip through Anatolia not long ago. Neither party understood much of the other's language, but they had exchanged cigarettes and melon seeds bought at the frequent halts. The Turks, to tease their guest, had made remarks that he did understand, to the effect that the U.S. had Cadillacs and atom bombs, that Russia had Sputniks, but that poor Britain had nothing. Nettled, the Englishman pointed at one wayside halt to a loaded donkey standing by the tracks. "Turkish Cadillac!" His joke was short-lived. The Turks' friendliness turning to nationalist wrath, they proceeded to beat him up.

Over much of their history the Turks have been pre-eminently a people of soldiers. In a durable impetus of energy they took over the fragments of two empires, the Arab and the Byzantine, and united them in a new empire, the Ottoman, which they held for several centuries with fearsome courage. On such modern battlefields as Gallipoli and Korea Turks have shown that they remain soldiers of unequaled tenacity. In Turkish comics, in Turkish films, in Turkish daily life, there is an exaltation of the warrior almost equal to that in the old Japan.

It is not only in comics and films that the Turks see themselves as soldiers. A large segment of their youth looks daily into a soldier's mirror, shaving before dawn in dingy barracks in the upland military towns. The Army—proportionately one of the world's largest—is omnipresent. Its sturdy, crop-headed conscripts, whose military qualities are the pride of every Turk and the admission of every enemy, slouch around city streets on their days off. Their walk seems an infinitely persistent shuffle. There

MODERN CITY of Istanbul is shown in blue on the map at right. Lying at the southern end of the Bosporus, the waterway that runs from the Black Sea to the Sea of Marmara, the city consists of five major sections. Two—Üsküdar and Kadıköy—lie in Asia. The European sections—Beyoğlu, Eminönü and Fatih—are divided by the Golden Horn, which is spanned by bridges (solid lines). The Asian and European sections are connected by ferries (dotted lines).

is none of the flashy militarism associated with the goose step. The pace of these underpaid warriors (after a military coup in 1960 their pay was increased by several hundred per cent to around a dollar a month) is in time with the movement of the Central Asian ponies on which, in folk migrations lasting through a millennium, their ancestors leaked west from the borders of China into the valleys, plains and uplands they were to make their own.

Assertions sometimes made in Turkey that every Turk regards military service as an honor and does not expect reward may be patriotic exaggerations. Many Turks dislike the rigors of military life, and many critics argue that a huge Army is a waste of money. Yet military values are totally accepted, and the military virtues are deeply valued. Turkish veterans will stop and show you—whether "you" are ex-enemy, ex-subject or ex-ally—a treasured wound from some resounding battle. The military virtues are more than bravado. They include steadfastness of spirit, as was shown in the Korean War, when not one out of hundreds of Turkish prisoners collaborated with the Communist enemy. Military élan may show itself less admirably in driving habits that litter the great new highways with burned-out buses and overturned trucks. A Turkish truck driver will not yield. On the highway, on the wrong side, he will not swerve.

The Turks have traditionally taken pleasure in a diversion enjoyed by warriors and civilians alike: eating. While the country does not concern itself with the sauces and intricacies of French cooking, Turkey can claim to be one of the world's great kitchens. The gourmet may not find great cooking, but the traveler will hardly find bad food anywhere. In the Middle East, Istanbul enjoys a renown similar to that of Paris in the West: Greeks, Egyptians, Syrians and Lebanese derive their standards from those set by the cooks of Bolu, a small town in Anatolia from which the rich families in the Bosporus palaces used to draw their cooks. But it is by no means only the rich Turks, who first delighted in such dishes as "lady's navel" (a circular pastry soaked in honey) or "the imam fainted" (a dish based on eggplant), who prize good eating. Someone selling a bus ticket in Istanbul for the distant journey from Trabzon to Erzurum will look up and say: "You will pass through the hamlet of Hamsi Köyü. It is about ninety kilometers [56 miles] up from the coast. There the bus will stop for twenty minutes, time enough for you to order *Sütlaç*. Nowhere in Turkey do they make goat's-milk pudding better." Weeks later the traveler's bus grinds through the mountains and stops at the shabby roadside café in Hamsi Köyü. He finds that what he had been told is precisely correct. The pudding is superb.

BESIDES being warriors and connoisseurs the Turks have been graceful builders, not only in Turkey but in places as far afield as Samarkand and Cairo, where such Turkish rulers as Ibn Tulun, Sultan Hassan and Qaitbay built masterpieces of mosque and tomb. Some of the best Turkish architects are claimed by other ethnic groups. There is much argument, for example, about the ethnic background of Sinan, a 16th Century master whose majestic religious buildings are matched by his practical yet elegant bridges. But this is to miss the point. Like the Arabs before them, the Turks were a people who absorbed others. They gave the dominant taste to a vast empire; they, as patrons, called the tune, paying the masons and choosing well. But as with other peoples their taste both as patrons and collectors

declined with time. The Topkapı Museum in Istanbul, which once housed the Sultans and their harems, and which now holds an unrivaled collection of clothes, embroidery, tiles and Ming celadon, shows in its buildings and in its treasures a melancholy transition from the simple and severe through the decorative to a flimsy ornateness which married Victorian fussiness with debility. Yet even when Turkish taste was decaying at the imperial center, the ordinary Turks knew how to situate towns and villages to the best advantage. Just as drab crowds in cobbled streets today seem lit up by the carnations they buy and carry, so the plains of Anatolia are dotted by villages where a mosque, a minaret and a sweep of poplars arrest the eye.

DESPITE disasters that would have destroyed a lesser people, despite the loss of an empire and violent seismic shifts in their fundamental beliefs, the Turks are today pressing forward—not geographically, as they did in the past, but in spirit. Within this century their leadership has chosen to move them West, en bloc—no longer to lead the Moslem East but, instead, to form part of the Western Christian community, without in so doing turning them into Christians. The Turks seem, in their haste to modernize, indifferent to their own past, unaware even of the virtues that they have always had. The outsider can only applaud the courage with which the new goals have been embraced. At the same time the contrasts seem equally significant to an assessment of Turkey. Naturally an ancient civilization cannot be changed overnight; naturally pockets of the old linger on; naturally there must be debate whether in certain cases the old should be maintained against a new whose novelty is not always proof that it is superior or right. The Turkish belief in the future—a belief that is still vigorous despite some setbacks—is admirable; but to the outsider the Turkish past is no less fascinating. For what makes Turkey uniquely interesting among modern states is the immense expanse between the *whence* and the *whither* in its historic pilgrimage. The Turks are the heirs of the Ottoman Empire, which in turn was the heir of a rich past; as their destination modern Turks have chosen the unexotic goal of democracy and egalitarian advance.

With the traditional dispenser attached to his back, a juice vendor finds eager customers at a wrestling field in the town of Edirne.

A People Deeply Attached to Ancestral Customs

After centuries of struggle in Europe in defense of the traditions and ideals of Islam, many of the people of Turkey have, within the last 50 years, embraced the values of their former enemies. But while the inhabitants of the larger cities have wholeheartedly accepted the "Westernization" begun by Kemal Atatürk in 1923, the great majority of Turks, who live in small, scattered villages, have scarcely been affected. In spite of Government-imposed changes in modes of dress and language, they retain an inner attachment to the religion and customs of their ancestors. Suspicious of city ways, they are occupied almost exclusively with the struggle for subsistence in the difficult terrain and climate of Asia Minor.

15

DINING OUT, businessmen are entertained by a singer and violinist at a popular restaurant near Istanbul. Just as Western standards of dress prevail among the clientele, much of the cooking is European rather than Turkish. Urban night clubs also offer Western dancing and entertainment.

WATCHING A PARADE in Ankara, holidaying Turks *(opposite)* gather on the base of the Confidence Monument to get a better view. The monument—which was commissioned by Atatürk—is designed to express the people's "patriotism, love of work and confidence in their destiny."

SMOKING A NARGHILE, or water pipe, an elderly Turk *(left)* peruses his newspaper in one of Istanbul's small coffeehouses, in which only men are allowed. Puffed in a very leisurely fashion, this ancient type of pipe passes the tobacco smoke through a water container to cleanse and cool it.

HISTORIC TOWN of Trabzon *(opposite)* lies by the Black Sea. Here, in 400 B.C., Xenophon and an army of fellow Greeks retreating from Persia reached the sea during the historic "March of the 10,000." Trabzon was also a Byzantine stronghold.

SOLITARY SHEPHERD on the central Anatolian plateau *(right)* needs only a rifle, a sheepcrook and a dog to pursue his age-old occupation. He is wearing a broad felt cloak which cuts the cold, dry wind that often blows across the open plateau.

CAMEL CARAVAN, carrying the possessions of a group of nomads, leaves a roadside camp and resumes its journey. Turkey has about two million nomads who live by breeding livestock. The Government discourages their wandering way of life.

MODEST VEIL, a holdover from centuries of use, is worn by a woman of eastern Turkey. Although Atatürk began a campaign against veils in 1925, he was successful only in the cities. Today they are still worn in the small towns and villages.

SITTING ON THE FLOOR, a family gathers for conversation in the morning. Rural society is becoming more open, but custom still forbids the social mingling of men and women.

ENDING THE WORKDAY, men of the town of Van crowd into a dim restaurant for supper *(left)*. Favorite dishes include *döner kebàp* and *şiş kebàp*, made with mutton grilled on a spit.

GLOWING AT DUSK, a shop in Antakya—formerly called Antioch—offers pastries and sweets. Turkey is renowned for such delicacies as baklava, a flaky pastry that is filled with nuts.

WARMLY DRESSED TOWNSMEN gather on a street corner in Diyarbakır to exchange gossip. There is little else to do; the pace of such eastern towns is slow.

SNOW-MANTLED MOUNTAINS dwarf a carriage crossing the fields near Erzurum in the eastern highlands, where cold weather usually persists far into the spring.

HOMEMADE SLEDS provide sport for the boys of Van in eastern Turkey *(below)*. Most other outdoor activities of the villages cease during the months of snow.

HIGH-PILED HAYSTACKS rest atop buildings which serve both as barns and dwellings in Erzurum. The climate of eastern Turkey is extremely inhospitable. Summers are arid and dusty. In spring and autumn, cold or hot spells strike suddenly. Transportation is paralyzed in winter, and wolves roam the countryside. Avalanches and earthquakes are not uncommon.

MIST-SHROUDED STADIUM erected by Roman engineers stands on the site of ancient Perga. Near the southern coast, Perga was a prospering town in Roman times. St. Paul made Christian converts there when he first arrived in Anatolia.

Previous Tenants

THE 31 million people of today's Turkish republic nearly all speak Turkish; language links them to some 30 million speakers of Turkish dialects in Central Asia, whence came the Turks who first entered Anatolia in the 11th Century A.D. Nearly all of Turkey's modern citizens share still another bond with other peoples: as Moslems they are linked to the Islam that stretches from Morocco in the West through North Africa and the Middle East to Pakistan and Indonesia in the Far East.

Yet important as are these extranational factors, Turkey draws its identity from a separate source—its Anatolian homeland. Modern Turks are a mixture of the varied peoples who have entered and settled in Anatolia over the last 8,000 years. This genetic and cultural heritage shows in the features and traditions of the people; the fact that Anatolia is one of the oldest areas of human settlement, a target for centuries of successive waves of newcomers, also accounts for the profusion of ruins with which the countryside is embellished, ruins that antedate the arrival of the first Turks by thousands of years.

Anatolia has in the main absorbed, rather than been conquered by, its invaders. The absorption of layer after layer of new arrivals shows even in the landscape of Anatolia, where the mud-brown villages often stand on hills. These hills were not all created by nature. They are the result of millennia of

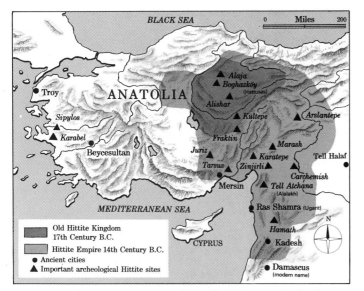

COMPACT EMPIRE established by the Hittites, the first known conquerors of Anatolia, is shown on the map above. From the 17th to the 14th Century B.C. their power was limited to the dark blue area. After the 14th Century they established a loose group of states that extended their control over a larger area *(light blue)*. A series of invasions finally broke up the empire.

rains deluging the earth-built houses in which the successive generations of Anatolians have lived. As the rains fell, a good deal of earth seeped down from the walls; and as the centuries passed, the successive house groups rose higher and higher on the debris of the past. These hills when opened up often reveal to the modern archeologist the deposit of history, layer on layer.

One such hill, at Catal Hüyük in southern Turkey, contains the remains of one of the earliest societies uncovered anywhere. A neolithic settlement, it flourished from about 6500 B.C. to about 5700 B.C., some 4,000 years before the first Egyptian pyramids were built. The Catal Hüyük culture was far from rudimentary, and its anonymous artists created a series of small but expressive figurines that testify to religious hopes. The dominant figure in the pantheon is a bulbous Earth Mother, symbol of fertility and the promise of food.

Although Catal Hüyük eventually perished, other neolithic communities based on the rearing of animals and the spasmodic sowing of crops spread across Anatolia. In time they came in contact with richer cultures to the south of the stern Anatolian plateau, in particular that of Assyria in what is today Iraq. At Kültepe, near modern Kayseri, the earliest documents in Anatolia have been uncovered. These were written by a colony of Assyrian merchants living peaceably among their Anatolian hosts, trading with them rather as a New York company's employees might today be trading in one of the developing countries of Africa or Asia.

The Kültepe tablets date from the 19th Century B.C., a period when the first great power to mold Anatolia was beginning to emerge. This power was that of the Hittites, a people who probably contributed more to the early evolution of Anatolia than did any other group.

Until relatively recently the Hittites were regarded as an almost mythical people, their only known historical figure being Uriah the Hittite, mentioned in the Old Testament account of David and Bath-sheba. Yet thanks to modern excavators the Hittites now stand revealed as a great and impressive people. Of the beginning history of Anatolia the British archeologist Seton Lloyd has written: ". . . the central historical fact is the existence for several centuries in the late second millennium of a great imperial power, centered on the [Anatolian] plateau, but extending its influence over much of the peninsula."

The synthesizing power that Anatolia has always exerted is detectable even among this early people. The names of the Hittite gods were Semitic, reflecting the strong cultural influence reaching into the peninsula from the great civilizations of Babylonia and the Middle East; at the same time the Hittites' language reveals that they were one of the Indo-European migrant groups that have created much of Western civilization.

The center from which the Hittites spread was located in central Anatolia, near the great bend in Turkey's longest river, the Kızıl Irmak, which was known to the ancients as the Halys. This is a rolling region of moderately fertile valleys and grass hills. The Hittite capital was Hattusas, now marked by the Turkish village of Boğazköy. The city's massive walls still stand; they have none of the delicacy of design shown by the temple walls of Egyptian Thebes, some of which were built during the same period. Nor can the Hittites' culture as a whole compare in subtlety and elegance with the richer manifestations of Babylonia and Egypt, from which it borrowed such motifs as sphinxes. At its best, however, Hittite sculpture has the tangled richness of Indian art. Something strong and idiosyncratic rises from the Hittite remains. At their empire's height the Hittite kings seem to have been more manly and less autocratic than the divine puppets who so often sat on the Egyptian and Babylonian thrones to the south. Just as their walls breathe an Anatolian severity and grandeur, so what we know of their history shows that the Hittite people were not only good soldiers but individuals endowed with a solidity which they seem to have bequeathed to the Anatolians of today.

FOR in dealing with the Hittites we are not dealing with people who came, then vanished. Their legacy affects all those who have lived in Anatolia after them. They were the first people to find the key to the haphazard puzzle of mountains which make a relief map of Anatolia so baffling. Present-day Turkish roads often follow the primitive network of communication worked out by the Hittites. Most important of all, the Hittites, with their widely scattered empire in Anatolia, provided much of the basic racial stock onto which later peoples became grafted. It is hard to define a "typical" Turk, but much of what appears typical of the Anatolian peasantry today seems to have a good deal in common with the stocky, roughhewn men whose features are preserved in the sculptured reliefs of Boğazköy.

When the Hittite state collapsed in the 12th Century B.C., after a series of weak rulers failed to deal effectively with pressures exerted by aggressive neighbors, a number of kingdoms rose and flourished in Anatolia. Their names resound yet: Lydia, for example, whose wealth and softness both were proverbial; and Phrygia, whose native headgear oddly became a world emblem of freedom. (The Phrygian bonnet can be seen to this day on the head of Marianne, the lady who symbolizes the French republic on its coins and bills.) Anatolia's new kingdoms were not large in size; their small scale is shown by the most famous of them all, the kingdom of Troy, which overlooked the narrows joining the Sea of Marmara to the Aegean in northwest Anatolia.

Its topless towers, its 10-year siege, its abducted Helen have made the kingdom of Troy a dominant force in the imaginations of men for nearly 3,000 years. The 19th Century rediscovery of the site of Troy quickened the living nerve of historical imagination; at the same time a visit to the complicated ant heap of superimposed cities gives, not disappointment, but a vivid douche of truth to those whose perspectives have been made grandiose by reading the *Aeneid* of the Roman poet Vergil or the *Iliad* of Homer. The city which epitomized "Asia" in that prototype of struggles between East and West is now a mere hillock in the plain which fronts the brilliant sea. All of the poets' facts are accurate: Mount Ida, still forested, rises behind Troy; the Island of Tenedos, which concealed the treacherous Greek fleet when the wooden horse was placed before Troy's gates, still exists; even the winds to which Homer so often alludes in his stock phrase, "wind-swept Troy," blow endlessly from the Aegean. What is inaccurate is the puffing up of fantasy in the minds of readers. Troy, Priam's proud capital, long-sought goal reached over the wine-dark sea by swift-footed Achilles, ambitious Agamemnon and crafty Odysseus, was, alas, not an imperial city but a village of some seven acres; the Trojan War must have been merely a bloodstained squabble between clans. The cruelty of Achilles in dragging Hector's body around and around the city walls under the eyes of the Trojan women is utterly credible, something a village ruffian could easily do with his rival, given a chariot and two horses. The wooden horse that was rolled through one of the village gates could have held only a handful of Greek warriors at most. But even a handful would have been enough to overpower the guards and open the portals of tiny Troy.

IF Troy symbolizes the small scale of the powers that shaped Anatolia in the centuries before Christ, other minuscule cities along the western coast —Pergamum, Smyrna, Miletus and Ephesus—symbolize the small fires from which the sparks of scientific method and inquiry leaped across the Aegean Sea into Greece, thence to ignite men's minds in the West as a whole. The philosopher Thales of Miletus argued that water was the original element from which everything came; Anaximenes, also of Miletus, preferred to consider air the basic source of life; Heraclitus of Ephesus added a more metaphysical view that all matter was constantly in a state of flux.

Hellenism, as the culture derived from Greece is called, was to play, in other forms, a vital role in the molding of Anatolia. Alexander the Great, himself a Macedonian although a pupil of the Greek philosopher Aristotle, conquered most of Anatolia in his great Fourth Century B.C. sortie into the East. Although Alexander's empire crumbled on his death, his lieutenants established a number of Hellenistic states in the Middle East. Seleucus, one of Alexander's successors, eventually came to rule over an empire that linked Babylonia and much of Anatolia. With its chief city at Antioch, the Seleucid kingdom—which endured more than two centuries—diffused Greek manners and ideas in the southern and western regions of the country.

The Hellenistic kingdoms eventually fell before the advance of another power. In the First Century B.C., Rome united the countries of the Mediterranean basin, including all of Anatolia, in one superstate. Greek influences remained dominant in Anatolia, however. The common culture of the Roman Empire derived more from Greece than Italy, and in its eastern sections Greek was used more commonly than Latin. In the Greco-Roman period Anatolia became one peaceful state for the first time. Rome was supreme on sea and land. Only a power with such over-all mastery could control the plateaus, the interior valleys and the complicated coastline of Anatolia. The Hittites had united the interior and had exercised some control over northern Syria and Phoenicia, but much of the Anatolian coastline had escaped their influence. Pamphylia, as the narrow strip of coastal land southwest of the Taurus was known, was so isolated before the Roman conquest that it had been a pirate base. When Roman naval power under Pompey broke the pirate empire based on Coracesium (modern Alanya), a rich Greco-Roman civilization

HOW ANCIENT TROY WAS FOUND

Through most of the 19th Century, scholars believed that Homer was a mythical poet and that the *Iliad*, the tale of the Greeks' war with Troy, was pure fancy. But a German businessman, Heinrich Schliemann, was convinced that Troy was a real place and the *Iliad* a true story. In 1868 Schliemann traveled to Asia Minor. In 1870, with about 100 workers, Schliemann began digging at Hisarlık in northwest Anatolia, a site he selected solely because it fitted the *Iliad*'s description of the site of Troy. By 1873 he had found nine ancient cities buried one on top of another. He picked the wrong level, the third from the bottom, as the Troy the Greeks had sacked, but proved that the city had existed. Subsequent scholars identified the Troy of the *Iliad* as the sixth level and produced further evidence that the *Iliad* tells of real events and may well have been written by a poet named Homer.

spread all along the southern coast of Anatolia.

The visitor to this part of Turkey today sees an astonishing chain of Roman ruins at such places as Aspendus, Sidé and Perga. Roman aqueducts that brought the snow water from the Taurus still stride through barren hills. At Sidé the ruins of a rich slave market glitter by the brilliant sea. In Sidé, as well as in Perga and Aspendus, large, open-air theaters capable of seating thousands stand almost intact near sites today occupied by slow-paced villages.

The culture disseminated by Rome was personified at its best by the Roman Emperor Hadrian, who ruled from 117 to 138 A.D. The Emperor traveled extensively in Anatolia and was a patron of many of its cities. In Bithynia, in the northwest, Hadrian discovered a young Anatolian named Antinoüs and made him a favorite. Idealized busts and full-length statues of Antinoüs, executed by the Emperor's sculptors, marked the beginning of the last creative period of classical sculpture. At the city of Pergamum Hadrian endowed a hospital-library. Pergamum's Aesculapium, a temple complex dedicated to the god of healing, provided methods of therapy startling in their modernity. On the outside portal of the Aesculapium was written the hopeful maxim: "Here only death is forbidden entrance." Inside, the priests of Aesculapius used techniques based on suggestion to cure illness. The drugged patient would be carried along a subterranean tunnel to a temple basement equipped with speaking tubes through which priest-doctors could whisper therapeutic advice. An obese patient, for example, would wake in the morning convinced that the god himself had recommended more exercise and less food. A small theater, as well as the books of Hadrian's library, provided recreation for the patients, while a gymnasium supplied the means for exercising their bodies.

But Hellenistic civilization offered its rewards to the rich and the powerful; to the slaves and peasants, who comprised the majority, it provided fewer satisfactions. During the period of the Roman peace, Anatolia was to acquire a spiritual view different from that of Hellenism, one which offered consolation to the oppressed. The apostle who brought Christianity to Anatolia was Paul, himself a native of Tarsus, a city in the Cilician plain south of the Taurus Mountains. Paul's missionary journeys started near modern Antakya, the ancient Antioch, where the followers of Jesus first became known as Christians. Paul carried the message of Jesus from one city to another in Hellenistic Anatolia. Tradition says that the Virgin Mary died in Ephesus on the west coast. The beloved apostle, the Gospel-writer John, lived there; it was probably another John who addressed Revelation, the last book in the New Testament, to the Seven Churches of Asia, early Christian communities on the coast and in the interior of Anatolia.

The upshot of the missionary work of Paul, the two Johns and their successors was the gradual transformation of an Anatolia with a Greco-Roman culture into an Anatolia that shared, with the rest of the Roman Empire, the rising new culture of Christianity. On the political level this Christianization reached its climax inside the empire in 330 A.D., when the converted Emperor Constantine transferred the capital of the empire from Rome to Byzantium. The shift in power from Rome in Italy to this new Rome on the Bosporus, renamed Constantinople in the Emperor's honor, inevitably put Anatolia in the center, where before it had been at the periphery. For at least seven centuries Anatolia was part of the heartland of the Christian Byzantine Empire. At Nicaea, a western Anatolian city nowadays shrunk to a village, Constantine summoned the first ecumenical council in 325. With the Emperor as

THE TRIALS OF THE ARMENIANS

Few peoples have known as many changes of fortune as the Armenians. Located in eastern Anatolia and extending eastward into what is now the U.S.S.R., Armenia was in ancient times a buffer kingdom between rival empires. Armenia was frequently invaded—by Assyrians, Persians, Arabs, Greeks and Romans. Withal, the Armenians retained their identity. In the 11th Century, after still more invasions of their homeland, a number of Armenians established a new kingdom on the southern coast of Anatolia. This kingdom in its turn was destroyed in the 14th Century by invaders from Egypt. Under the Ottoman Empire, Armenian merchants and financiers thrived. As the borders of the empire contracted in the 19th Century, however, struggles broke out between Turks and Armenians for the possession of Anatolian lands. Many Armenians died; others fled abroad.

chairman the bishops defined the nature of Christ's relationship to God. The basic creed of the modern Roman, Anglican and Orthodox Churches is still called the "Nicene."

Yet western Anatolia had not been the first region of the peninsula to be converted to the new faith. In 301 King Tiridates III of the eastern Anatolian state of Armenia, who had been converted by St. Gregory the Illuminator, had announced that henceforth Christianity was to be the Armenian state religion. Armenia was one of the most ancient entities in the world. Successively overcome by Babylonian, Persian and Roman invaders, the Armenians had stubbornly refused to submerge themselves in their conquerors' empires.

Now that all of Anatolia shared one faith it might have seemed probable that the Armenians would coalesce with the other Anatolians. This did not happen. While the conversion to the new faith cut Armenia off from the neighbor to its east, Zoroastrian Persia, it did not unite that ancient and idiosyncratic nation with the other Christians of Anatolia. The Armenians demonstrated their independence when they refused to accept the doctrinal decisions of the Council of Chalcedon, which expanded the Nicene Creed in 451.

The disunity of the Christians, their disputes over dogmatic details and their readiness to plot against one another were to be factors undermining the permanence of Christian civilization in Anatolia. In addition, the pretense of the Christian emperors in Constantinople to be not merely wielders of power but also quasi-religious figures as the first Christians of the realm must have alienated many when these same emperors acted, as they often did, with total disregard for gospel precepts.

Byzantine power was, moreover, weakened by extraneous factors. Western Christian Crusaders must take much of the blame for the fact that Anatolia was to cease to be a Christian territory—and, in fact, to become a stronghold of a new, monotheistic religion: Islam. On their road to the Holy Land the Crusaders had marauded and looted; the crowning damage to the Byzantine fabric came in 1204, when the feudal leaders of the Fourth Crusade sacked the sacred city of Constantinople.

The shift from Christianity to Islam therefore seems in retrospect readily explicable. Toward the end of the Middle Ages, Anatolia repeated the experiences of North Africa, another great area of the Roman Empire which had changed into a base for the rival religion of Islam after years as a Christian stronghold. In North Africa a colonial Roman aristocracy had dominated an indigenous peasantry; a similar situation had existed in Egypt, where the peasants had been oppressed by a Byzantine upper class based on Alexandria. These submerged groups had shown their will to self-assertion by espousing heresies that showed promise of being able to damage Rome. When the Arabs invaded North Africa in the Seventh Century, their new religion of Islam had spread rapidly among the peasants; imperial Christianity collapsed like a card house.

The fall of Byzantine Christianity was to take place less rapidly in the home province of Anatolia, but with equal finality. The Anatolian masses became more or less indifferent to the question of who would rule them next. Islam was to spread easily in ensuing years among peasants who had never understood the niceties of Orthodox theology and who disliked their oppressive Byzantine lords.

YET though doomed to run out, the Christian centuries were nevertheless to leave a lasting impress upon the land and people of what is now Turkey. In architecture the heritage is particularly evident. One of the distinguishing features of the mosques that crown the Istanbul skyline is the dome, the development of a form used by the Byzantines in their small and large churches alike. Equally lasting was the Byzantine effect on Anatolian social customs. The Christian empire had lasted so long that its way of life, its attitude toward women, even its cooking habits had come to be taken for granted and as such were adopted by future generations. Later

Byzantium was not the fossil it has sometimes been portrayed to be. Art flourished up to the end, as did some forms of popular piety. As late as the 14th Century the strange, lunar valley of Göreme was still populated by hundreds of Christian hermits who carved cells and churches into the easily worked, porous rock. This kind of monastic piety was to become transmuted under a different but still monotheistic creed in later centuries, when Anatolia was to spawn a unique profusion of Moslem religious orders. Again, the diplomacy that had been an essential skill of the Byzantines—particularly as their pretensions to being the New Rome became supported by less and less power—was also to be a feature of the Ottoman power that was to inherit Anatolia.

THE next phase in Anatolian history—the Turkish—has continued until today. The Turks, like other newcomers before them, have blended with the Anatolians they found on the peninsula. There have been periods of tranquillity, periods of violence. In their slow absorption of Hittite, Greek and other elements the Turks have conformed to the conditions imposed by a terrain where lightning conquests have been rare and where the pace of history has more often resembled a trickle than a spate. The Turkification of Anatolia (see Chapter 3) has been a slow process, taking almost 1,000 years to accomplish, and it is still not complete. While the Greeks have either been absorbed or expelled, while comparatively few Armenians still live within the Turkish republic's frontiers, a few million Kurds in southeast Anatolia have not yet coalesced with their Turkish-speaking fellow Moslems. The Kurds are a people who speak a language akin to Persian and who claim descent from the Medes mentioned in the Bible.

If the Turks have been one more strain among many, they have also been the dominant strain which more than any other has made Turkey what it is today. The language and the Moslem religion that the Turks brought with them when they moved into the country have become the language and the religion of the vast majority of Anatolians. Yet while providing the dominant element in a country that rightly takes its name from them, the Turks themselves have been modified by the Anatolian traditions and peoples that they have superseded.

In massive stone Antiochus I surveys the mountains of central Turkey, where he ruled a small kingdom in the First Century B.C.

Long-fallen Testaments to Transitory Greatness

Turkey's past is a palimpsest—a slate written upon and repeatedly erased through the centuries. Archeologists can see the shadows of once-great cultures in Stone Age pottery, Hittite temples, and Greek and Roman cities. The first known conquerors of Asia Minor were the Hittites, who arrived in Anatolia about 2000 B.C. and flourished for eight centuries. After the Hittites' fall, Greeks eventually colonized the Aegean coast. The Greek outposts fell to Persians; the Persians were conquered by Alexander the Great; and after Alexander's empire disintegrated, Romans took most of the peninsula. Rome and its offspring, Byzantium, lasted until 1453, when Constantinople fell to the Ottoman Turks and almost five centuries of Moslem rule began. Today the myriad armies, religions and languages that once gripped Anatolia survive only in the neglected buildings that conquerors erected in testament to transitory greatness.

31

HITTITE TEMPLE, lined with sculptured soldiers, is set in a hillside 100 miles east of Ankara. The Hittites conquered the indigenous Hatti people in 2000 B.C. and ruled much of Asia Minor and Syria for 800 years.

CARVED HIEROGLYPHS of Hittite priests *(left)* long defied deciphering. In power and culture the Hittites rivaled the contemporary civilizations of Egypt, Babylonia and Assyria. They were conquered by the Assyrians.

MOUNTAINSIDE TOMBS, believed to be copies of dwelling houses, contain the remains of long-dead Lycians *(opposite)*. Inhabitants of southwest Anatolia, the Lycians were conquered by invaders again and again.

RUINED EDIFICES *are all that remain of the ancient colonies of Greece and Rome*

FORLORN PEDIMENT of a temple in Ephesus stands on a rubble-strewn hillside. Ephesus was founded by Greeks in the 11th Century B.C. and later became a Roman provincial capital.

TOPPLED RELIEF of Diana, goddess of the hunt, rests in the remains of a Roman theater at Sidé *(below)*. Sidé, on the southern coast, was a flourishing trade center under the Romans.

ROAD OF MARBLE, the Arcadian Way at Ephesus runs 1,700 feet from a city square to the silted-up harbor. The Romans rebuilt the road after gaining control of the city in 133 B.C.

THE STREETS OF EPHESUS are now tilled by Turkish peasants *(left)*. Ephesus boasted one of the seven wonders of the ancient world—the large and magnificent Temple of Artemis.

TEMPLE OF AESCULAPIUS, god of medicine, is marked by its round walls *(below)*. It is located in Bergama, the ancient Pergamum, which was a center of learning in classic times.

STALWART FORTRESSES, their
masters vanished, overlook
once-strategic hilltops and approaches

GUARDIAN OF A HARBOR, Korigos Castle *(above)* stands on an island near the seaport of Mersin in southern Anatolia. It defended the coast of a kingdom known as Little Armenia.

A CONQUEROR'S STRONGHOLD, Rumeli Hisar Castle commanded the Bosporus when it was built by Sultan Mehmet II in 1452, the year before his capture of Constantinople.

HILLTOP BASTION, the fortress of Yılan Kalesi looms over an Anatolian valley *(below)*. It was built by a King of Little Armenia, Leo II. Despite such awesome defenses Little Armenia had a short lifetime. The kingdom was established in the 11th Century; in 1375 conquerors from Egypt destroyed most of its towns, and Little Armenia disappeared from history forever.

Establishment of an Empire

THE modern state that is Turkey is in many ways an amalgam of the disparate traditions of two distinct peoples. One of these groups traces its origins to the Arabian desert that lay at the frontiers of the Christian Greco-Roman empire; the other came from the Central Asian region on the frontiers of China. The two groups were to interact upon each other. The Arabs, the first group, were to give Turkey its faith; the Turks, the second, were for long to give the Arabs their rulers.

While the Arabs were fanning out from Arabia in the Seventh and Eighth Centuries, the Turkish peoples outside the Great Wall of China were moving west. The Arab desire to exchange a desert for fertile land was powered by a new religious faith, the stern monotheism of the Meccan merchant Mohammed. Islam, as "submission" to Mohammed's message was called, claimed to be the last clear restatement of the perennial Semitic faith whose earlier messengers had included Moses and Jesus. The Arabs, pagans lightly influenced by a trickling of Jewish and Christian ideas, submitted to the new prophet's message with volcanic fervor and within one generation after their conversion to it had surged out of Arabia to the frontiers of Tunisia in the west and of Afghanistan in the east.

The Turkish migrations were prompted by less forceful impulses. From time immemorial, pastoral peoples of Central Asia had migrated westward when their pastures became arid or when they were threatened by more aggressive tribes. Like the Huns who came before them or the Mongols who came after them, the Turkish nomads had been affected by the great culture beyond the Wall of China. Here lies a parallel with the Arabs and their rudimentary awareness of Jewish and Christian ideas.

THESE original Turkish migrations were unplanned. There was no set intention to conquer or rule, either in the name of an ideology or a racial ambition. The Turks were a simple, virile people, priding themselves on their honesty and horsemanship, their courage and loyalty. They lived by selling their services to others, by raids, by small-scale war. No racial prejudice prevented their marrying the daughters of other tribes.

The first Turkish leader to make a mark on history—and to give his name to a whole phase of Turkish expansion—was Seljuk. During the 10th Century, Turks who came to be known as Seljuks reached the southern part of what is now the Uzbek region of the Soviet Union. The single most important event to take place on the westward journey was the conversion of the Seljuk Turks to Islam. This conversion took place during the Ninth and 10th Centuries, when the Turks were still beyond the Oxus River in a region ruled by Moslem Persia. If this event was important to the Turks, it was hardly less so for the world they were to affect. Other groups living on the Eurasian steppe were converted to Christianity; they were to create modern Russia. Others embraced Judaism. In accepting Islam the Seljuk Turks, among the most redoubtable people to come out of Central Asia, embraced the duty laid on every Moslem to propagate his religion, by force if need be. In accepting that obligation they did so with the dedication that was always their hallmark; in later centuries the descendants of other migrant groups from Central Asia were to feel the weight of Turkish devotion to Islam.

The missionary effort for Islam was still in the future. The Turks first set foot in Anatolia in 1048, in what seems to have been a casual raid. They invaded not the territory obedient to Byzantium but Armenia, the buffer state between that power and

Persia. Although both the Armenians and the Byzantines were Christians (with certain doctrinal differences) the bond of a common faith did not rally the two peoples against a common danger. To their mutual detriment both states were to regard each other, rather than their tough new enemy, as the major peril. Anatolia had had Arab Moslems on the frontier for several centuries and had managed to put up with them. Neither the Armenians nor the Byzantines were sufficiently alarmed by this new force on the Middle Eastern scene.

The Arab Moslems to the south were well aware of this new Turkish element in the house of Islam. In the first flush of Islamic success the Arabs themselves had founded an empire that eventually stretched from Spain to the borders of India and welded almost the entire Middle East into one power.

The Arab dynasty that achieved this vast success was known as the Umayyad. Based on Damascus in Syria, the Umayyads claimed to be caliphs, or successors to Mohammed. After a century of Umayyad rule another dynasty, the Abbasid, seized control of the Arab empire and of the title of caliph. In 762 the Abbasids moved east and made Baghdad their capital. The Abbasid empire weakened, however, after reaching the peak of its power under Caliph Haroun al Rashid in the Ninth Century; the decline coincided with the arrival of the Turks.

UNABLE to rely on their factious Arab subjects, and faced with the growing military might of Persia, the Abbasid caliphs turned with relief to the Moslem Turks—swordsmen who were only too willing to serve as mercenaries to the most glittering court in the world. But the caliphs rapidly fell under the influence of those who served them. As early as 836 Caliph Mutasim had to move his capital from Baghdad to Samarra, a city he founded farther north on the Tigris, because of constant brawls between the Arab citizenry in the old capital and his Turkish bodyguards. Gradually the Abbasid caliphs lost control of Spain, North Africa and Egypt. The Abbasid Caliph al-Qaim recognized the new situation in a fragmented Middle East in 1056 when he granted Seljuk's grandson, a leader named Tuğrul, the title of Sultan—an Arabic word meaning "he with authority"—while retaining for himself a caliphate whose

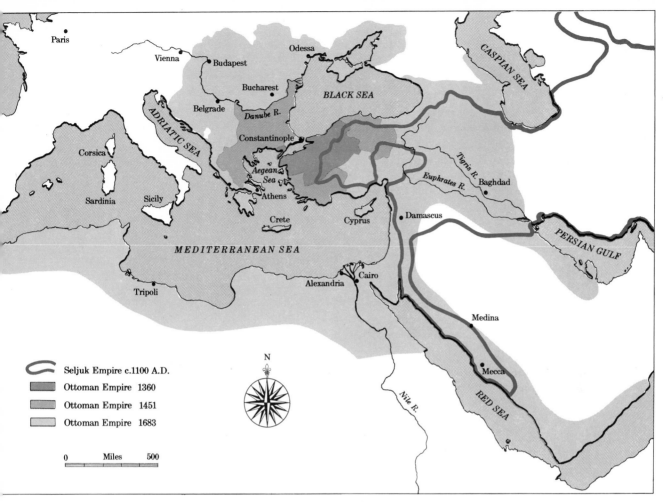

EXPANSION AND DECLINE of two Turkish empires, the Seljuk and the Ottoman, are indicated on the map above. Established in the 11th Century, the Seljuk Empire had by 1100 A.D. gained control of much of Anatolia and regions to the east and south *(solid blue line)*. Later, it entered on a gradual decline. The Ottoman Turks settled in eastern Anatolia during the 13th Century; by 1360 they had vastly expanded their territory and begun expansion into Europe *(darker blue area)*, taking Constantinople in 1453. In ensuing centuries the Ottomans pushed deeper into Europe and Africa. After a final assault on Vienna in 1683, the empire gradually contracted until all territories outside of Anatolia and the Istanbul region were taken away.

meaning was now nebulous. This shift of power into the hands of Turkish Sultans was eventually to take place outside the Abbasid domains as well. After 1250 the rulers of Egypt were all non-Arabs of Turkish descent.

The Seljuk Turks were successful on other fronts as well. In 1071, under their leader Alp Arslan, their armies overwhelmingly defeated the Byzantines at the Battle of Manzikert. This was the decisive battle in the Turkification of Anatolia. After this victory the whole of Anatolia lay open to Turkish settlement; the opportunity to advance and settle was taken and in a few years the Seljuks had reached the outposts of Constantinople and had established a capital at Nicaea.

Alp Arslan was in many ways an enlightened ruler. As Sultan he refused to employ the Arab-style *sahib-haras*, a kind of secret police whose function was to spy on potential enemies of the ruler and to execute those condemned to death. Alp Arslan's reasons for rejecting a secret police have been reported. If "I appoint a *Sahib-khabar* [police spy]," Alp Arslan said, "those who are my sincere friends and enjoy my intimacy will not pay any attention to him, nor bribe him, trusting in their fidelity, friendship and intimacy. On the other hand my adversaries and enemies will make friends with him and give him money; it is clear that the *Sahib-khabar* will be constantly bringing me bad reports of my friends and good reports of my enemies. Good and evil words are like arrows; if several are shot, at least one hits the target. Every day my sympathy to my friends will diminish and that to my enemies increase. Within a short time my enemies will be nearer to me than my friends and will finally take their place. No one will be in a position to repair the harm which will result from this."

ANATOLIA under the early Seljuks was a loosely united territory. But under Sultan Alaeddin Keykûbat, who reigned from 1219 to 1236, most of what is now Turkey was united in a tolerant, pluralistic kingdom in which Christians and Moslems served in a common Army. The heavily fortified naval base of Alaiye (Alanya) contained an elaborate dockyard tunneled into the cliffs of the harbor, and a massive bastion called the Red Tower, which still stands. Seljuk society valued the craftsman. Even Sultan Keykûbat knew the arts of carpentry, calligraphy, draftsmanship and bowmaking. He may have learned them in the jail in which he had been imprisoned by his brother and predecessor to prevent his seizing the throne prematurely.

Under Keykûbat, Anatolia knew stability for the first time in centuries; communications were as secure as they had been under the Roman Empire. Caravansaries, or inns, were established on the main roads, each one at a distance from the next that a laden camel could cover in nine hours—that is, about 18 miles. Many of these caravansaries still stand in Anatolia. They were used as late as the 17th Century, when an English merchant described one at which he stayed: "They are built in fashion of a cloister, encompassing a court of thirty or forty yards square. . . . At these places all comers are free to take shelter, paying only a small fee . . . and very often without that acknowledgement."

Good communications helped commerce to flourish. Commercial wealth made possible the establishment of what might be called a welfare state. Schools, endowed hospitals in which free treatment was available to the poor, orphanages and poorhouses made the 13th Century a period in Islamic history when the charitable precepts of Mohammed were translated into rules of action, not pious exhortations.

The single greatest figure produced by this tolerant, syncretic civilization was probably Celaleddin Rumi, a poet and mystic. Rumi—the surname derives from Rum, the name generally given to Anatolia in Seljuk times—was brought as a child to Keykûbat's capital of Konya from Balkh in Afghanistan. His major poetical work, the *Mesnevî*, runs to 26,000 couplets and has been described as a Moslem *Divine Comedy*, since it is an attempt to interpret the whole of human life in Sufi, or mystical, terms. Its first couplet stresses the sense of alienation that all mystics feel when confronted by the phenomenal world:

> *Listen to the reed, how as flute it makes lament,*
> *Telling how once from the reed-bed it was rent.*

Rumi was not simply a poet, and the name "Mevlâna" (Our Master), as he is known to modern Turks, testifies to his role as a spiritual guide. A man of fascinating personal attraction, Rumi surrounded himself with disciples called dervishes, whom he taught doctrines that often approached pantheism. "I am the mote in the sunbeam," he wrote. "I am the ball of the sun; I am the glow of morning; I am evening's breath." A soul in love with God, Rumi used dances already known among certain mystical brotherhoods as a means of reaching another, higher level of consciousness; in a whirling dance enacted to the tune of a flute the worshiper achieved an approximate absorption in the unity of God. "What can words do for me?" Rumi makes God declare to Moses in one of his writings. "I want a glowing heart. Inflame hearts with love and disregard thought or wording."

THE mystical movement of which Rumi was a supreme exponent was not created in Anatolia; it had flourished for some centuries in Persia and the Arab countries. The movement put down its deepest roots in Turkish Anatolia, however, a reflection perhaps of the fact that one side of the Turkish character is mystical and otherworldly.

Despite its glories, the Seljuk state was to disappear. While commerce had flourished, while the stores of city merchants had been well guarded, the frontiers of the state were far from secure, and the fields of the peasantry frequently were overrun and ravaged by marauders. As the Seljuks softened into a civilized, urban people, a new invasion from the east, that of the Mongols, was to devastate Seljuk Anatolia.

Only six years after Keykûbat's death in 1236—reputedly, he died of poison administered by his own son—his people suffered a crushing defeat by the Mongols at Kuzudağ. The whole peninsula lay open to attack. Yet even then the machinery of history was preparing the next round.

The passage of the Mongols had disturbed many Turkish tribes in the east, tribes still basically nomadic but converted to Islam and having a vested interest in Turkish civilization. One of these tribes was the Kayi. According to legend, the 400 families of the tribe chanced in the 13th Century to arrive on the scene of a battle between Mongol and Seljuk forces. No Turks could resist a battle, and the chivalrous Kayi threw their support to the Seljuks, who were losing the fight. Under their leader, Ertuğrul, they turned the tide in favor of the Seljuks. In gratitude for the timely intervention of the Kayi the Seljuk Sultan presented the wandering tribesmen with territory near Eskişehir in western Anatolia, an area contiguous to the frontier of the diminished Byzantine Empire.

IN the small town of Söğüt, Ertuğrul's wife in 1258 bore a son who was named Osman. Under Osman the tribe rapidly expanded its territory. Osman died in 1326, unaware that he was to give his name to the greatest and longest-lived of Turkish dynasties. Known to the East as Osmanlıs, to the West as Ottomans, the descendants of Osman were to unite the greater part of the Mediterranean and the Middle East under one rule. Almost incidentally they were also to accomplish the next stage in the Turkification of Anatolia.

Asia had often produced military geniuses. The extraordinary achievement of the Ottomans was to combine military genius with patience, and a talent for civil administration with imperial *élan*. In the words of the British historian Edward Creasy: "It is indeed a remarkable trait in the character of the first princes of the Ottoman dynasty, that, unlike the generality of conquerors, especially of Asiatic conquerors, they did not hurry on from one war to another; but, on the contrary, they were not more eager to seize than they were cautious and earnest

---

UNIQUE FEATURES OF THE OTTOMAN WORLD

Distinctive institutions of the Ottoman Empire attracted great interest in Europe. The following three were among the best-known, often through highly romanticized accounts.

THE SERAGLIO: A term applied by Turks to the Sultan's entire household, court and palace, the word was used by Europeans to refer specifically to the elaborately organized women's quarters within the palace. The Seraglio was ruled by the Sultan's mother, who supervised a vast array of disciplinary and administrative officers, as well as eunuchs who were held responsible for security. The women who lived in the imperial harem—sometimes numbering as many as 1,200—were mostly slaves and were rarely bound to the Sultan in legal marriage. Most, in fact, never even reached his chambers.

THE SUBLIME PORTE: This was the high-flown European translation of the Turkish term *"Babıâli,"* meaning "High Gate"—a reference to the residence of the grand vizier. Since most of the Government's administrative work was handled at the *Babıâli*, the term "Sublime Porte" became synonymous throughout Europe with the Ottoman Government.

THE "DEVSIRME": A term that means "collecting," *devşirme* stood for the practice of drafting Christian boys for the empire's military and civil service. Every three to five years, levies would be placed on unmarried Christian males between the ages of eight and 20 in the conquered states of Rumelia, Greece, Serbia, Bosnia and Hungary. They were taught Turkish, trained in Moslem ways and eventually added to the ranks of the Janissaries—an elite group of troops who were the personal slaves of the Sultan. Until the middle of the 17th Century the highest nonreligious positions in the empire invariably were awarded to Christian-born slaves who often became men of great power.

---

to consolidate. They paused over each subdued province, till, by assimilation of civil and military institutions, it was fully blended into the general nationality of their empire. They thus gradually molded, in Asia Minor, an homogeneous and a stable power; instead of precipitately heaping together a motley mass of ill-arranged provinces and discordant populations."

The Ottoman Empire in its prime was more like a self-perpetuating, self-enlarging corporation, a corporation devoted to the promulgation of an idea, than the usual empire in which a group of outsiders dominates conquered subjects. The Ottoman state from the start turned those it conquered into members of its own corporate body, into its own executives. This process can be seen as early as the reign of Osman's grandson, Murad I, who formed an elite corps of soldiers who came to be known as Janissaries. Their name in Turkish meant "new troops." A cross between the guardians of Plato's Republic and the Praetorian Guard of the Roman emperors, the members of the Janissary corps were recruited from the strongest and most agile Christian children in the empire. Converted to Islam, given many privileges, the Janissaries formed a standing army a hundred years before any such body was to be organized in Europe.

EVEN before this incomparable military machine had been forged, the Ottomans had expanded into Europe. In 1354 their forces left the sylvan Ottoman capital of Bursa, set among poplars and vineyards to the south of the Sea of Marmara, and crossed the Dardanelles to capture Gallipoli. Under Murad the Ottomans expanded their hold on Europe and made their second capital, Adrianople (now called Edirne), a businesslike advance post for Balkan conquest. Bayezit I, nicknamed "The Lightning" because of his rapidity of movement, seemed at the zenith of success in Europe when the empire was attacked in the east by Mongols led by Tamerlane the Great. Bayezit was forced to rush to the support of his beleaguered forces. His defeat and capture at the hands of Tamerlane was a stern blow to the Ottomans—though not a fatal one.

Under Mehmet I (1413-1421) and Murad II (1421-1451) the empire was reintegrated, the Turkish domains in the Balkans were expanded to the frontiers of Austria and Hungary, and the stage was set for the final destruction of Byzantine power by Mehmet II. In 1453 Mehmet earned the sobriquet "The Conqueror" by taking Constantinople from the Byzantines. Under the Conqueror's grandson, Selim I, the Ottoman Empire, which until then had assembled conquests from territories previously Christian, invaded and captured three centers of earlier Islamic power: Damascus, Baghdad and Cairo. With these conquests came the overlordship of the two holy cities of Mecca and Medina, as well as possession of many sacred objects belonging to the Prophet and his companions.

The Ottoman Empire continued to expand by acts of war. Its cohesion and its ethic lay as much in war as in the empire's dedication to the cause of Islam. Yet a curious feature of the Ottoman regime was its appeal to many of the people on its frontiers. Turkish conquests were often immensely facilitated by pro-Ottoman sympathies among the subjects of the feudal powers the Turks were attacking. The Ottoman yoke was often consciously preferred to that of an existing tyranny.

During the 16th Century, for example, the island of Cyprus was under Venetian rule. The Venetians treated the Greek-speaking islanders like European serfs. In 1563 a number of Cypriots, led by their priests, contacted the Ottomans and asked them to put the island under their care. (The priests had probably been impressed by the authority given to the Orthodox patriarch in Constantinople—an authority considerably greater than that allowed by the last Byzantine Emperor, himself a convert to Rome.) When the forces of the Ottoman Empire landed in Cyprus in 1570 they met with the support of many Cypriots, whose pro-Turkish sentiments were reinforced by last-minute atrocities committed by the Venetians.

At the same time that the Greek priests of Cyprus were deciding that they preferred "the turban of the Turk to the tiara of the pope," multitudes of Hungarian peasants farther north burned down their cottages and fled from feudal rule to Serbia to put themselves, their wives and animals under the rule of the Ottomans, whose head tax on non-Moslems was a light burden compared to what they had previously paid to their feudal masters.

UNDER the reign of Süleyman the Magnificent (1520-1566) the Ottomans possessed not only the best organized military force on earth—the most modern in its technology, its commissariat and treatment of its troops—but a society that was modernist and tolerant compared with those of contemporary Europe.

While it would be idle to call Süleyman a democrat, his empire was much more classless than other societies of the day. The Sublime Porte, or entrance to the council chamber of the grand vizier, the Sultan's chief minister, was thronged by carefully educated youths chosen for their promise and promoted on their merit.

For a variety of reasons the kind of hereditary aristocracy that was to be such a feature of European states for the next few centuries had little chance to thrive in Ottoman Turkey. In the first place the Sultan's autocracy tolerated no such baronial class of near-equals as had surrounded and limited the weak monarchies of medieval France and England. The Sultan reigned like the sun. With the exception of members of the royal family everyone in the imperial administration was but a slave of the Sultan. The Turkish word for slave, *kul*, was regarded not as an insult but a badge of pride. A "slave household" of 80,000 men became, after careful selection and severe training, the rulers of an empire.

A SECOND factor was the egalitarian element in Islam that emphasized that all men were subject to the laws of the Almighty. The *Seyhülislam*, or chief interpreter of the laws of Islam, carried great weight with the Sultan. When Selim I, a confirmed bigot, decided in 1514 to follow one campaign against Moslem heretics in Anatolia with another designed to force Anatolian Christians to recant or face the sword, he was opposed by a *Seyhülislam* named Jemali, who pointed out that under Islamic law such "peoples of the Book" as Jews and Christians had the right to preserve their faiths in security, provided they paid a tax. Selim, despite his epithet "The Grim," bowed to Moslem law and the Christians were left unharmed.

As for the Janissaries, the prohibition on their marrying, which was effective until the 16th Century, prevented their becoming an aristocratic caste. At the same time they acted as an effective check on the Sultan's absolute power. Sometimes this check was used for militaristic purposes, as in 1525 when the Janissaries pillaged the houses of Ottoman officials in order to persuade the Sultan to abandon his hunting vacation and get back to war. On other occasions the Janissaries raised an uproar in opposition to wasteful practices or unpopular favorites.

The Ottoman state was designed for every contingency except prolonged peace. Even royal fratricide, the worst vice of the Ottomans, was justified in governmental terms. The Koranic verse, "Disquiet is worse than killing," was quoted by commentators, and Mehmet II, Conqueror of Constantinople,

once stated: "To whichever of my sons the Sultanate may pass, it is fitting that he put his brothers to death for the sake of the order of the world. The majority of the jurists have approved, so let them act accordingly." The Conqueror's own murder of an infant brother was comparatively mild. When Murad III, reportedly the father of 103 children, died in 1595, his heir, Mehmet III, murdered his 19 surviving brothers; seven female slaves who happened to be pregnant were put into sacks and drowned.

Yet this legalization of the act of Cain—basically so that the state should be free from the wrangles of pretenders—was to ruin the dynasty it sought to serve. It is asking much of heaven to provide great talents in one family in every generation; it is asking preposterously much to ensure that these talents should be passed through a single brother. The loss to the descendants of Osman in the constantly repeated massacres of male children is incalculable. The greatest Sultan, Süleyman, had no brothers to kill. But under the influence of a beloved Russian wife who wished her own progeny to come to the throne, he agreed to the murder of Mustafa, his first-born son and a young man remarked for his talents and integrity. On his way to an audience with his father, Mustafa entered the royal tent to find not Süleyman, "but the seven Mutes, the well-known grim ministers of the blood-orders of the Imperial Man-Slayer. They sprang upon him, and fastened the fatal bow-string round his throat, while he vainly called for mercy to his father, who was in an inner apartment of the tent."

THIS crime could not even be justified by its results. Süleyman was succeeded by Selim II, son of his Russian wife, a man overly fond of the non-Moslem custom of drinking. The Turks gave him the sobriquet "The Sot."

If the Ottoman state owed its inception and much of its success to the abilities of the earlier Ottoman rulers, its decline can be connected with the later enfeeblement of the dynasty. After Süleyman's death, during his last campaign against Austria in 1566, there was to be no sudden collapse. But for three and a half centuries the Turks were to be forced on the defensive—an anguished posture for those who were most themselves when on the attack.

A National Creed of Strength and Honor

The virtues of strength, fearlessness and honor enjoy high esteem in modern Turkey. The Turks cherish their historic stature as a race of conquerors and annually re-enact the moment in 1453 when the Byzantine capital of Constantinople fell before "the sword of Islam." With Soviet Russia as a neighbor the maintenance of military might is a national necessity, and the Turks take great pride in their tough, virile soldiers. Especially in sport—wrestling and the horseback game of *cirit*—the determined, aggressive character of the Turkish people shows through.

COSTUMED CHILDREN playing band instruments march past the wall of Istanbul during a 1964 restaging of the 1453 battle in which Mehmet II, "The Conqueror," took Constantinople.

MOCK STORMING of Constantinople's walls draws a huge crowd *(left)*. Staged during the quarrel with Greece over Cyprus, the 1964 ceremonial battle had a particularly ferocious tone.

TURBANED TROOPS file back from the "battle" to join a parade *(opposite)*. The victory in 1453 came after seven weeks of siege and a final assault in which thousands were killed.

STRAINING WRESTLERS, their muscles taut beneath the sheen of olive oil, search for each other's weakness during a contest in Edirne held annually for more than 600 years. Wrestling has always been the favorite Turkish sport. Turks perennially win in international competitions, and they can wrestle in almost any style. The tradition of oiling their bodies is an ancient one.

HIGH-RANKING OFFICERS point out troop movements during war games held outside Istanbul in 1964. The Army is a major force in Turkey. Constantly modernizing, it absorbs about 40 per cent of the national revenue. Every fit male youth must serve in the military.

ALERT INFANTRYMEN stand a field inspection during 1964 maneuvers (*below*). Turkey's military establishment numbers up to 400,000 men. The Navy has at least 10 submarines; the Army is equipped with motorized artillery; the Air Force boasts some 300 U.S.-made jets.

*RUGGED HORSEMANSHIP is
a requirement for a swift-moving
game called "cirit," popular
in the eastern highlands*

BRANDISHING STICKS, teams spur their ponies wildly across a snow-covered field *(right)* during a *cirit* match. A game of daredevil riding, *cirit* is played by two teams of five horsemen each. The wooden sticks are thrown at the opposing riders. Each hit is worth one point.

GALLOPING DOWNFIELD, a *cirit* player charges the opposing team *(below)*. When a stick is thrown, a rider must return to his own side for another, thus attacks are rarely made in concert. Real *cirit* skill lies less in throwing than in agile maneuvering of the quick ponies.

POISED FOR THE THROW, a rider *(above)* twists his pony in a tight turn toward an opponent. The *cirit* rider—unlike a polo player—does not wear a protective helmet.

CELEBRATING VICTORY, jubilant teammates do an impromptu folk dance *(below)*. *Cirit* is played only in winter, when there is no farm work to be done.

CIRCLE OF MEN spins dizzily *(above)* during one of the movements of a popular peasant dance being performed at a festival held in 1964 at Rumeli Hisar Castle near Istanbul.

GLIDING COUPLE gestures in another dance at the festival *(below)*. Each region of Turkey has its own dance styles. In some areas men and women are forbidden to dance together.

SOLITARY PERFORMER enlivens a Sunday morning *(above)* in the southern town of Gaziantep, as Gypsy musicians accompany him. Turkish folk dancing is extremely varied: peasants

perform dance pantomimes of such everyday events as sifting flour or spinning thread; they mimic combat (with and without weapons); they imitate eagles, bears, cranes and even such natural phenomena as flowing rivers or poplar trees in motion; they dance with drums and wooden spoons. Most dances are performed by groups, but some, like this one, are solo displays.

Sultan Abdül Hamid II, a ruthlessly repressive Ottoman ruler, rides a carriage through Constantinople. He was deposed in 1909 by

...oung Turks, a group of reform-minded and militant nationalists.

4

Sick Turks, Young Turks

LIKE many other long-lasting institutions, the Ottoman Empire gave rise during its twilight years to clichés of phrase and attitude among its neighbors. Yet paradox, that characteristically Turkish figure, must modify two of the best-known phrases: "the sick man of Europe," which was used to describe the Ottoman Empire in its last years, and "Young Turks," the term given to the radicals who, it was thought, were renovating that empire in the early years of this century. The Ottoman sickness was one of those chronic maladies where the victim outlasts his physicians. And instead of renovating the empire whose sickness they diagnosed, the Young Turks killed it.

The Ottoman sickness had not been confined to the Seraglio, although the Sultans' palace, with its immense, walled harem, was a popular image of attraction and repulsion. The first 10 Sultans were as remarkable, as rulers, as were those produced by any political system anywhere; the later Sultans, with only a few exceptions, have been well described by the British historian Bernard Lewis as a series of "incompetents, degenerates and misfits."

In the first half of the 17th Century Murad IV became the last Sultan to lead his armies in a victorious campaign. His successors were content to luxuriate at home and to leave the expansion and the maintenance of the frontiers of Islam to others. Shortly before Murad had come to the throne the custom had been established of keeping the young Ottoman princes virtual prisoners, isolated in separate quarters so as to prevent fratricide. Such a custom was not calculated to produce energetic or confident rulers.

IN many states the dwindling of the monarch to a constitutional figurehead could have been a sign of progress. In Britain, for example, the diminution of the monarchy in the 18th Century preceded a great period of British expansion. No such development followed the retrogression of the Ottoman sultanate. By the end of the 17th Century the empire had reached its territorial limits. Murad had been militarily successful, but his victories were gained in Persia, a zone which was actually of secondary interest to the Ottoman state. The primary zone had always been Europe; the early Sultans had conquered the Balkans before they became masters of all of modern Turkey. The western limit to expansion into Europe was fixed at Vienna during the 16th Century reign of Süleyman the Magnificent and confirmed in the following century. The last vain assault on Vienna took place in 1683.

In many states the stabilization of a frontier, the acceptance of a final limit, could have been a blessing. The end of territorial expansion could have opened the way to economic and political consolidation within the stabilized state. This was not the case with the Ottomans. Their state had been born in the fighting zone between Islam and Christianity; seeing themselves as missionaries, and Europe as a mission field, they had expanded into the Balkans with the aim of eventually converting the whole of Europe to the faith of the Prophet.

The compulsion to stand still revealed fundamental weaknesses. Since the state was geared to its military machine, booty had provided much of its wealth. Ottoman leaders envisioned wealth in nonproductive terms, valuing collections of jewels or furs. In an economic sense the Ottoman system was comparatively nonproductive. "In the military empire, at once feudal and bureaucratic, which they had created," writes Bernard Lewis, "the Muslims knew only four professions: government, war, religion and agriculture. Industry and trade were left to the non-Muslim conquered subjects, who continued to practise their inherited crafts." When the Ottoman Empire could no longer expand, the economic productivity of the changing European nations gave them an inestimable lead. This lead kept the Ottoman Empire on the defensive throughout the 18th and 19th Centuries. The finances of the empire were chaotic; the value of its currency was in constant decline. Its once-magnificent bureaucracy became corrupt and inefficient. A society once devoid of a landed aristocracy was overgrown by a caste of feudal lords who ruled the countryside of the empire.

YET despite the loss of a province here, a dependency there, the empire hung on. Its surprising survival was not the result of the efforts of the Padishah, or "ruler of rulers," as this grandiloquent title for the Sultan means. The empire survived because of the tenacity of the ordinary Ottomans, who constantly surprised Austrians and Russians by the fervor with which they continued to fight. Their willingness to battle was not simply a matter of bravery; it was linked to something else: the very real sense in which the Ottoman ideal retained the allegiance of millions of Moslems. To them the empire still represented the "house of Islam." Connected with this factor was another: the ability of this Islamic state to secure and hold the services of great administrators, many of them European converts to the tolerance of Islam. Some great viziers, or ministers, rose from the humblest positions; Mehmet Köprülü, an able 17th Century Grand Vizier of Albanian origin, had started his career as a cook boy.

Still another factor was, in the long run, of paramount importance to the Turkish future. Ottoman society was not the petrified jungle that the West sometimes imagined it to be. A continuing series of critical intellects began suggesting remedies for the empire's problems as early as the 17th Century.

These would-be reformers did not belong to one school, nor were they uniformly impressed by Europe. Some were conservatives, arguing that the state had weakened not because it had failed to modernize and change but because it had not adhered to its original pattern.

YET with the passage of time most of the critics adopted a modernizing stance. For in an area where the Turks were particularly sensitive, Europe was shown to hold an increasing advantage. This was the battlefield. Ottoman soldiers, never deficient in courage, began to find themselves outclassed in weapons and effectiveness by the armies of once-despised infidels. The stimulus to reform came more and more from a will to catch up, not so much with Western Europe as with a Russia ruthlessly modernized by Peter the Great.

The need for internal and external reform became urgent at the end of the 18th Century. The accession of Selim III to the Ottoman throne in 1789 was followed by two outstanding events: the start of the French Revolution and a catastrophic Turkish defeat at the hands of the Russians in the Crimea. In his desire to meet Russian threats Selim was to be impressed, instructed and indirectly destroyed by French influence.

The Janissaries, who had been the guides, guards and administrators of earlier Sultans, became, correctly, the first target of Selim's renovating zeal. Swollen from Süleyman's devoted 20,000 to nearly 150,000, they had become a bigoted caste scattered throughout the empire. They were inefficient in war, troublesome in peace. Selim tried to induce them to accept French training. When they refused, he established the Nizam-ı Cedid, a rival army corps organized on European lines. Selim also had time to establish military and naval colleges staffed by French officers. The colleges' primary aim was to give instruction in gunnery, fortification and navigation, but the French instructors inevitably inculcated their students with liberal thoughts; the result was the formation of cadres of young men aware of new ideas.

In 1798 Selim was mortified when Napoleon succeeded in invading Egypt, nominally a province of his own empire, although in fact long ruled by the Mamelukes, a self-perpetuating caste descended from slaves originally imported to administer and guard the estates of the Egyptian Caliph. Despite his admiration for all that Napoleon represented, Selim had sent a force to help his Mameluke subjects. One of the leaders of this force was Mohammed Ali Pasha. Mohammed Ali established a virtual kingdom for himself in Egypt after massacring the Mamelukes. As an autocratic modernizer Mohammed Ali was also the pacesetter for Selim's cousin Mahmud II, who came to the Ottoman throne in 1808 after the Janissaries had dethroned Selim. Selim's successor was Mustafa IV. Mustafa was in turn deposed by Selim's supporters, and was succeeded by Mahmud. As the new Sultan, Mahmud was the wiser for his cousin Selim's experience with the Janissaries and the example set by Mohammed Ali on dealing with the Mamelukes. Mahmud did not move against his Janissaries until he had established a corps of artillery devoted to himself. The Janissaries rose in protest in their ritual of revolt: they upset their huge iron soup kettles. Always in the past this clamorous action had culminated in the Janissaries' getting their own way, whether their demands involved the execution of an unpopular vizier or a new cash donation to themselves. This time it led to surprises. Mahmud's artillery was focused on the Janissary barracks. When the angry Janissaries assembled, thousands of them were shelled to death. Mahmud then set about developing a modern army and a centralized bureaucracy under his direct control.

MAHMUD may well have seen himself as a Turkish Peter the Great. He recognized, like Peter, that radical changes were required in society. He showed this in other than purely military ways. In the Topkapı Museum in Istanbul a visitor today sees striking evidence of the abruptness of Mahmud's changes. In a gallery displaying royal robes—the dark blue silk of Süleyman, the brilliant hues of Bayezit II—there is a sudden break. The last Sultan to be remembered by a turban and robe is Selim III. Mahmud's costume is a pair of red-striped blue trousers and a blue cape. Among his subjects Mahmud introduced something daringly new—the red fez which replaced the turban, the traditional emblem of the pious Moslem. The acceleration of reform can be seen in the fact that a century later this revolutionary headgear was itself to be abolished as the symbol of reaction, for after Mahmud the debate over reform was to continue through phases that would lead to total revolution.

THE ideas of Europe were to be destructive as well as constructive in their impact on the Ottoman Empire. One idea associated with the French Revolution—nationalism—was to work havoc in the multinational society held together by Ottoman power. The idea that each national group was entitled to political independence was alien to orthodox Islam and orthodox Christianity alike; the idea that a quasi-religious enthusiasm should be expended on a national cause was not only new but heretical. Yet this explosive idea found fertile soil in the Ottoman Empire, particularly among the empire's many Christian minorities. The peoples of the Balkans and the Levant had been placed under one roof by the Ottoman Sultans, but they had not been united. While those who embraced Islam enjoyed full Ottoman status, other religious groups known as millets, or nations, were permitted to preserve a certain autonomy in the conduct of their affairs; they obeyed their own religious leadership. These undigested groups had coexisted under the Moslems with fair contentment throughout the centuries, although their status was second-class and their security depended on the Moslem principle of tolerance.

The introduction of nationalist ideas—picked up from contact with Napoleon's invaders and from diplomatic missions to Europe—spread hope among the millets that separation from Ottoman control and full sovereignty might be obtainable. For some —the Serbs, Bulgars and Greeks—hopes of independence were to be realized. For the Armenians scattered throughout the empire independence was not to become a reality; the nationalistic efforts of their leaders led only to massacre and dispersion for thousands.

The infusion of nationalist ideas was to complicate the task of the "Young Ottomans," as the reformers within the empire came to be known, for the success of nationalism among the empire's millets was to rule out certain reformist solutions that might otherwise have been practicable. While most Turkish reformers became more and more persuaded that the strength of the West lay in constitutional freedom, not merely in firepower, their efforts to liberalize the Ottoman Empire tended to hasten its disintegration. The only innovations that were safe were such technical inventions as the telegraph, which could be used to bind the scattered Balkan and Arab provinces closer to the center. But to copy such Western institutions as parliamentary democracy or a free press was likely to have disruptive results. Instead of binding the various millets to the Sublime Porte, a free press inevitably would have made them more conscious of their differences, while the granting of the vote might have resulted in the separation of the restive millets from the empire.

AN experiment in political democracy nevertheless was attempted as the result of the workings of liberal ideas among the small but growing educated class. On December 23, 1876, the Ottoman Empire responded to those ideas by promulgating a Constitution. The Grand Vizier, or chief minister, was Midhat Pasha; the Sultan who endorsed the Constitution was the supposedly liberal Abdül Hamid. The Constitution guaranteed certain limited rights to Ottoman subjects and established a parliament; by a stroke of the pen it seemed that Turkey was to take its place among the nations ruled by representative assemblies. But in little more than a year the Sultan intervened, dismissed the new parliament, suspended the Constitution and exiled Midhat, who was subsequently jailed. The Ottoman Empire was now once more ruled by a despot; to the liberals among his subjects Abdül Hamid seemed the personification of reaction.

In the sense that Abdül Hamid set himself against the liberal trend of the century he was certainly a reactionary; the Sultan was also in his own way an innovator, although his innovations were material and technical rather than democratic. By suppressing all debate, by keeping all power in his own hands, by creating a large secret police, Abdül Hamid managed to hold his empire together. What he could not do was hold the allegiance of the young, educated Ottomans. Many Ottomans had become aware of Western liberal movements; as students, diplomats or exiles they had visited European capitals and seen the functioning of parliamentary governments that allowed considerable freedom of criticism and political organization.

The reformers of Abdül Hamid's youth were called Young Ottomans; the reformers of his old age came to be known as Young Turks. While the Sultan's tyranny lasted on into the 20th Century, the Young Turks lived in an atmosphere of hopeful conspiracy. At least four distinct ideological threads (often entangled) were each acclaimed as the escape line from the despotic labyrinth.

The first of these threads was Ottomanism. It postulated loyalty to a renovated plural society presided over by the Ottoman Sultan, but one in which all persons—whether Moslem or Christian—would enjoy equal rights as citizens under a constitution. The nonreligious aspects of Ottomanism were of themselves admirable. But a dedication to Islam had been one of the major cohesive forces of the empire. It might be doubted that a secular Ottomanism lacking the emotional power of religion could have held the loyalty of minorities evidently eager for separation.

A second group of idealists recognized that the main power of the empire had indeed derived from its identification with Islam, which remained the most compelling force in the feelings and judgments of Moslem Ottomans. This group espoused the Pan-Islamism preached by Jamal al-Din al-Afghani, a fiery revivalist who preached that all Moslems should unite in one state. Depressed by the overweening success of the Christian West, the Pan-Islamists comforted themselves with a vision of the glorious Islamic caliphate which in medieval days had been superior in power and culture to the West.

But Pan-Islamism would have faced as many problems as had Ottomanism. Its espousal might have boldly alienated the Christians and Jews of the empire. Its espousal would also have involved the Ottoman Empire in even more clashes with the West, for a major proportion of the world's Moslems were subjects of the British King or the Dutch Queen.

The label "Young Turks" suggests the direction in which much Ottoman thought was moving. For almost a century the empire had been at the receiving end of revolts and wars caused by other people's nationalism. If there could be Greek, Bulgarian and Armenian nationalism, why not Turkish?

Once this idea was accepted the question arose of what, in terms of nationalism, a Turk was. The two answers suggested to this question contributed the third and fourth threads.

A GROUP known as Pan-Turanists argued that all those who spoke a Turkish dialect, as well as all those who belonged to something vaguely defined as "the Turkish race," belonged to the Turkish nation, wherever they might live. But advocating the inclusion of "all Turks" in one nation-state had implicit perils. The adoption of Pan-Turanism might have alienated Moslems like the Kurds and the Arabs, who hitherto had been loyal supporters of the state. At the same time Pan-Turanism could only have increased enmity with Russia, which included half the world's Turkish speakers among its subjects.

The fourth thread was known as the "nationalist movement," or Turkism: a concentration on the Turks who lived inside the Ottoman Empire. This meant, in effect, the Turks of Anatolia. In its theoretical form, while the empire still existed, this doctrine had disadvantages, implying, as it did, the abandonment of non-Turkish territory as well as the pretensions of the Ottoman caliph to a spiritual role in the whole Moslem world. The Young Turks rejected Turkism; ironically, the doctrine represented the best hope for Turkey, and it was the one

TWO WHO TRIED TO REFORM AN EMPIRE

A few statesmen tried to infuse the declining Ottoman Empire with progressive Western ideas. In 1876 one such leader, the Grand Vizier Midhat Pasha, persuaded Sultan Abdül Hamid to promulgate a Constitution and convene a parliament. Shortly thereafter, however, the Sultan revoked the Constitution and banished Midhat. Another powerful reformer was Enver Pasha, a leader of the Young Turks, a group that fought against the corruption of Abdül Hamid's administration and brought about his dethronement. But Enver made the mistake of taking Turkey into World War I on the side of the Central Powers, a move that ended the Ottoman Empire.

MIDHAT PASHA

ENVER PASHA

that was eventually to save the country a generation later.

In 1908 the Young Turks finally achieved power. They brought off a military coup and announced the restoration of the 1876 Constitution. When Sultan Abdül Hamid tried to organize a countercoup he was at last deposed and replaced by Mehmet V. The new leaders included a group of Young Turk intellectuals, a few millet leaders and some progressive officers. Known as the Committee of Union and Progress, they aimed at transforming the Ottoman Empire into a constitutional monarchy.

But the coup set in motion a historic landslide that was to bury the Young Turks' idealistic aims, and out of the four contending philosophical threads only Turkism would remain as a feasible escape route. While inside the Ottoman frontiers, the Young Turks' victory promised liberal advance; outside those frontiers the overthrow of Abdül Hamid offered a promising opportunity for the enemies of the empire to close in for the kill. The Young Turks had no time to consolidate constitutional advance; they were at once faced with concerted attacks by Greek, Serb and Bulgarian rebels in the Balkans, and in 1911 Italy invaded Tripoli, the last Ottoman possession in North Africa.

UNFORTUNATELY for the Young Turks their arrival in office had coincided with a change in the traditional balance of power in Europe. The emergence of imperial Germany had led to a rapprochement between France and Britain, Turkey's allies in the Crimean War, and Russia, the empire's most persistent enemy. The insecurity of the diminishing and demoralized empire was a factor in the internal transformation of the Committee of Union and Progress into a dictatorship led by three men: Enver Pasha, Talât Pasha and Cemal Pasha. Of the triumvirs, Enver Pasha was pre-eminent over Talât Pasha and Cemal Pasha. When the two rival empires of Austria and Russia became entangled in World War I, Enver Pasha brought the Ottoman Empire into the struggle on the side of the Central Powers. This disastrous miscalculation was to produce the final disintegration of the Ottoman Empire; in this disintegration atrocities and counteratrocities were to make any long-term solution based on revived Ottomanism or Pan-Islamism totally unthinkable.

One great victory was to stand out in a chapter of disgrace and defeat. It was secured by Mustafa Kemal, an officer later known as Atatürk. He had opposed the involvement with the Central Powers. His victory was all the more impressive—and therefore all the more therapeutic to Turkish morale—in that it was secured against the flower of the British Empire at Gallipoli, the jugular of the Turkish state.

But everywhere else the Ottomans shared defeat with their German allies. The triumvirs scattered: Talât to Germany, where he was assassinated; Enver and Cemal to Russia, where both died violently.

HALIDE EDIB, one of the first Moslem women to assume a role on the Turkish national scene, witnessed the despair of those days when the Young Turk leaders fled and Sultan Mehmet VI failed to lead. On May 16, 1919, a friend told Halide Edib that Greek invasion forces had landed at Smyrna the day before. "Nothing mattered to me from that moment . . ." she wrote later. "I suddenly ceased to exist as an individual: I worked, wrote and lived as a unit of . . . magnificent national madness." The empire already had lost its Balkan and Arab provinces. A plan to partition Anatolia among the victorious Allies was now being put into effect.

A few weeks later Halide Edib, accompanied by her niece, went to the open space outside the Blue Mosque in Istanbul. There she addressed a crowd of 200,000 people in an effort to rally national support against the invaders. As the meeting broke up —a meeting that was to be one of thousands as Turkish consciousness exploded before the threat to the very concept of Turkish autonomy—Halide saw an old man crying aloud and raising his hands to the sky. A middle-aged woman, very shabby but strong-looking, was running like a girl, shouting: "He has come to us! He has come to us!" Exhausted from her speech, Halide asked her niece *who* had come. Her niece, equally excited, told her: "The padishah . . . the sultan!"

But it was a false hope. The descendant of the Conqueror of Constantinople was nursing a headache in his palace at Yıldız. A monarchy that had lasted for six centuries was not to play even a nominal role in Turkish fortunes any more.

Light snow swirls around workers near the Galata Bridge, a link across the Golden Horn that divides the city's European section.

The Inexhaustible Variety of a Many-faceted City

The greatness of Istanbul, whose fabulous history is evident at every corner, remains undiminished to this day. Straddling two continents and connecting two seas, Istanbul is a city of many faces. Among the splendors of Ottoman mosques and Byzantine palaces are heard the murmured prayers of Islam's faithful, the cries of street vendors, the hooting of commuter boats and freighters, and endless discussions of business. Istanbul handles the predominant share of Turkey's banking transactions and maritime trade. With its web of waterways and innumerable fine restaurants, it remains a magnet to Turks.

61

SIMPLICITY AND URBANITY, in
constant ebb and flow, alternate
in the life of the nation's largest city

TOWERING ARCHWAY leads to Istanbul University, which occupies what was once the Ottoman Empire's War Ministry. Founded in 1453, the university today has 23,000 students.

JUMBLED ROOFTOPS cluster together in Istanbul's Beyoğlu section. The rest of the city's European section is across the Golden Horn. The Asian section is across the Bosporus.

WATERFRONT RESTAURANT along the embankment of the Sea of Marmara draws businessmen with its fresh seafood. Istanbul's citizens spend many nonworking hours near the water.

FRUIT VENDOR offers to weigh cherries at an open-air food market *(below)*. Vendors of vegetables, yogurt and even drinking water still cry their wares through the crowded streets.

A MARITIME FLAVOR pervades daily life in a city whose people are in frequent contact with the sea

BOSPORUS FISHERMEN stand on the embankment of the Golden Horn and advertise their catch to passersby. Hundreds of the city's citizens take their living from the nearby waterways.

WATER-BORNE COMMUTERS read newspapers as their craft *(below)* churns down the Bosporus past the Asian shore of Istanbul. Many businessmen maintain residences on the Bosporus.

RUSH HOUR in Istanbul's harbor *(above)* produces a dense and dangerous aquatic traffic jam. Its strategic position between Europe and Asia has made Istanbul a major port for centuries.

HOMEWARD-BOUND PEDESTRIANS, clad in the Western-style clothes now common in Istanbul *(opposite)*, cross the Galata Bridge. The signs advertise such products as radios and gum.

EMBARKATION POINT, the eastern side of the Galata Bridge serves as a dock for the ferries that make the run across the Bosporus to the Asian section of Istanbul. The bridge's lower level is crowded with restaurants, stores and smoke shops that commuters frequent.

JAGGED SKYLINE of Istanbul, seen from the Sea of Marmara, is topped by the needlelike minarets of the Blue Mosque *(above).* At the right is a portion of the sea wall that used to serve as a bulwark against naval invasions. The original city was once encircled by walls.

INTRICATE METALWORK decorates the Galata Bridge *(left).* A thoroughfare by day, the bridge draws crowds of sightseers at night.

with wharves that handle a thriving shipping traffic, serve as the city's vital arteries

TRANQUIL HARBOR, the Golden Horn winds below the hill of the Eyüp cemetery. The headstones bear carved fezzes to denote the graves of males and rounded stones carved with lotus leaves to mark female graves. The name of the waterway derives not only from its quarter-moon shape, but from its color at sunset and from the riches it has produced over the centuries as a harbor and fishery.

67

*RETREATS from the
pressure and pace
of the city are within easy
reach of its inhabitants*

RESTING IN THE SUN, visitors sit near the huge Blue Mosque *(opposite)* in Istanbul. Since the anticlerical campaigns instituted by Atatürk in the 1920s and 1930s, the religion of Islam has undergone a revival in this "city of 500 mosques."

HUNTING FOR SEATS, vacationers in Emirgan, a town on the Bosporus shore, crowd into an open-air restaurant *(above)*. In summer the temperature in Istanbul often soars above 95°, and citizens prefer to be near the cool Black Sea breezes.

RIDING IN A CARRIAGE, visitors to the Princes' Islands in the Sea of Marmara enjoy a simple summer holiday *(left)*. The islands, located about 12 miles southeast of Istanbul, preserve their peaceful atmosphere by prohibiting all automobiles.

PICNICKING IN A GROVE, vacationers cavort on the Princes' Islands. The nine islands are dotted with villas and gardens where carnations and other flowers are cultivated. The islands' population increases in summer from 15,000 to 40,000.

Atatürk: The Stern Physician

MUSTAFA KEMAL ATATURK, creator of modern Turkey, died of cirrhosis of the liver in Dolmabahçe Palace in Istanbul shortly after 9 a.m. on November 10, 1938.

The anniversary of his death provides the most solemn moment of the Turkish year. All over Anatolia, school auditoriums are draped with black. Under yellowing chestnuts, statues are festooned with flowers. The central rite takes place in Ankara at the great stone mausoleum where Atatürk's remains are buried. This shrine, perhaps the one impressive building in modern Turkey, has little in common with the tombs of the Seljuk or Ottoman rulers. There is something deliberately pre-Islamic in the great approach road frowned upon by squat lions. The resonant tomb chamber itself strikes no religious note. A large sarcophagus confronts an open window; a permanent bronze wreath overlays its base. To this sarcophagus on November 10 pace the inheritors of the regime that Atatürk created: president, prime minister, Cabinet ministers, judges, important soldiers, each carrying one garland to place atop the metal wreath. Precisely at 9:05 a trumpet sounds and everyone stands silent for five minutes. In one corner of the shrine a radio announcer whispers into a microphone.

The five minutes are not the end of the reverence paid to the departed leader. In flyblown mountain cafés as well as in city hotels, in barracks as well as in banks, in schools as well as in frontier posts, the face of Atatürk mesmerizes a generation that had hardly been born when he died, and that would hardly understand many of his speeches, so much has Turkish changed in the years since he began the reform of the language. The face is square, stern; the blue eyes are broadly set above high cheekbones; the lips are thin. But even these deified eyes would surely smile when on his anniversary drink is rarely served in restaurants and cafés as a tribute to the man whose own carousings brought him premature death at the age of 57. When he was a boy known only as Mustafa a schoolmaster followed a Turkish custom and gave him a second name, Kemal, or "Perfection"; now that he is dead his people have forced perfection on his life.

IN the surname granted him by the Turkish assembly—Atatürk, or "Father Turk"—this man was proclaimed one of the father figures of the century. What makes the man unique is the respect that is accorded him so long after his death, so long after he can neither bless nor hurt. His picture, not that of the current President or Prime Minister, is the central totem of the modern Turks. Mustafa Kemal Atatürk has been spared the downgrading of other fathers.

Atatürk's life was lived among events and scenery that might have been manipulated by some Olympian playwright to ensure that his hero knew the whole gamut of late Ottoman experience. This gamut was mostly a bitter one. When Mustafa was born in 1881 to lower middle-class parents in the Macedonian city of Salonika, there was nothing exceptionally fortunate about being a Turk. Mustafa's parents, Ali Rıza and Zübeyde, thought of themselves as Turks; whether they were in fact full-blooded Turks or whether, like so many other inhabitants of racially mixed Macedonia, they had strong admixtures of Slav or Albanian blood is impossible to ascertain, since the Ottoman Empire was the least racially minded of all states. But by being Turkish-speaking Moslems in largely Greek-speaking Salonika, the members of Mustafa's family were *ipso facto* identified with the Ottoman state whose rule was being increasingly contested by its subject peoples. If the

boy, trained to be proud of his status as a Moslem subject of the Sultan, raised his eyes to a map, looking for comfort elsewhere in the Ottoman world, he would have found little. The once-mighty empire had shriveled; its Government had become despotic and corrupt.

Like many of the leaders of the Young Turk movement (see Chapter 4), Atatürk was to be a nationalist from the periphery, his national pride sharpened by his daily contact with people who were not Turks and who disliked them.

A further spur to the young man's slumbering ambitions must have been the humble position of his family and the early death of his father. After resigning from his job as a Government clerk Ali Rıza twice failed in business, took to drink and died of tuberculosis when Atatürk was only seven. Left virtually penniless, his mother took the boy and his younger sister to live with an uncle on a nearby farm. Atatürk disliked the life and at the age of 12 overrode his mother's opposition and chose the Army for his career. In the empire of the time the choice was a wise one. The Army still represented power and prestige, two things to which Atatürk was never to be indifferent. To a young man without financial resources the Army schools offered one road to social advancement. At the same time arms represented the traditional profession and glory of the Turks, and the sentimental core in the granite of the future revolutionary burned for the Turks as such, the submerged race in a polyglot empire, not the dynasty that ruled them.

IN 1902 Atatürk was commissioned a lieutenant and assigned to the Staff College in Istanbul. There he and other young officers formed a secret committee and began distributing a handwritten newspaper attacking what Atatürk later called "evils in the administration and politics of the country." The newspaper was suppressed, but no action was taken against the young officers by the college superintendent, who, like other Army men of the time, was not completely in sympathy with the Sultan's Government. In 1905 Atatürk was graduated from the Staff College and commissioned a captain. Still in Istanbul awaiting assignment, he and a few other newly commissioned captains took to studying and discussing underground books attacking the Government. The young officers were denounced, briefly imprisoned and then sent to remote posts. Atatürk was assigned to Damascus in Syria. There, fighting Druse rebels, he received his first taste of action.

In 1908—the year of the Young Turks' revolution and only three years after Kemal had been graduated from the Staff College—Austria seized the two Ottoman provinces of Bosnia and Hercegovina, Crete voted for union with Greece, and Bulgaria proclaimed its independence. In 1911 Italy invaded Tripoli and Cyrenaica, the last Turkish possessions in North Africa.

Ten millrace years—in which his actions eventually gleamed against a background of general defeat—prepared the young officer to lead his people. Those years formed his notions of what long-term remedies would be required for the salvation of Turkey.

In 1909 Atatürk was a chief of staff in an army that marched on the capital from Salonika to suppress a counterrevolution against the Young Turk movement launched by the reactionary Sultan Abdül Hamid. The following year, having put down a revolt in Albania, he attended military maneuvers in France. In 1911 he was with the Turkish forces in Cyrenaica that attempted to repel the Italian invasion, and in 1912—a year of severe Turkish defeats at the hands of Montenegro, Serbia, Bulgaria and Greece—Atatürk participated in an unsuccessful attempt to relieve Adrianople, which was under Bulgarian siege. During 1913 he served as a military attaché in Sofia. He opposed the empire's precipitous entrance into World War I in 1914 on the side of the Central Powers not only because he disliked and mistrusted Germany, but because he believed that it might lose the war. In 1915 he defeated British Empire forces at Gallipoli in the one great Turkish victory of the war, and in 1916 he recaptured Bitlis and Muş from the Russians. By then he had

been promoted to the rank of general and given the title of Pasha. In 1918 Atatürk prevented the Turkish retreat from the empire's Arab provinces from becoming a rout. He then returned to Istanbul, the one Turkish leader who was not associated with defeat, as the Allied fleets entered the Bosporus. Soon Allied forces occupied the city and moved into portions of Anatolia. Under secret wartime agreements they had already resolved to divide the territory of the Ottoman Empire among themselves.

From 1919 to 1923 Atatürk was to be the major inspirer of what history may regard as the war of Turkish survival. On May 15, 1919, a Greek army protected by Allied warships landed at Smyrna, clearly intending to detach the western provinces of Anatolia from Turkish rule. The Greeks had entered the war only in 1917; this last humiliation at the hands of a once-subject people was too much for patriotic Turks to endure. Four days after the landing Atatürk arrived in the Black Sea port of Samsun, having been assigned by the Sultan to oversee the demobilization of the remnants of Ottoman forces in eastern Turkey. Nominally the Sultan's agent, he saw

THE ADOPTION OF FAMILY NAMES

Until the 20th Century most Turks had no last names. They followed the Moslem practice of using one name, given at birth, relying on a patronymic or a word indicating some special attribute for more precise identification. In 1934 Atatürk's regime ordained that all Turks take family names. His assumed name, Atatürk, means "Father Turk." The Prime Minister, Ismet, chose Inönü, the name of the town where he had won a victory over Greek forces in 1921. To avoid confusion, 20th Century Turks in this book are identified by the surnames they chose, even in passages describing their actions before Atatürk's law came into effect.

his own purpose as the organization of Turkish resistance. For some time Atatürk maintained the fiction that he was acting on behalf of a patriotic but impotent Sultan, that in rallying the Turks of Anatolia against the Allied invasion he was doing what the Sultan would have commanded had he been free of Allied pressures. But in truth Atatürk's departure from Istanbul represented a radical break with all that the capital on the Bosporus represented. His efforts to rally Turkish resistance showed rapid results. Newly created resistance groups met in conventions at Erzurum and Sıvas. Under Atatürk's guidance they produced a national pact that demanded the preservation of Turkey's national independence and territorial integrity. They vowed armed resistance against the occupying forces if their demands were not met. The small, centrally located town of Ankara was chosen as the center from which to unite Anatolia and expel the foreigners.

As time went on events more and more discredited the weak-willed Sultan, whose main concern appeared to be only the preservation of his throne. After the British occupation forces in Istanbul had arrested some prominent Atatürk sympathizers in the Ottoman parliament, the Sultan dissolved the parliament in an effort to appease the Allies. He also launched an all-out attack upon Atatürk's nationalists, sending an army to Anatolia to fight Atatürk's forces and ordering the *Seyhülislam* to declare that it was the religious duty of all Moslems to kill the rebels. A special tribunal was convened in Istanbul, and it passed a death sentence, *in absentia,* on Atatürk and his associates. At the same time, as if to give Atatürk's followers the proof they needed of the Sultan's abjection, the Allies forced his Government to sign the humilating Treaty of Sèvres on August 10, 1920.

Under the terms of the treaty the Ottoman state renounced sovereignty over the Arab provinces. In addition the Ottoman Government agreed to surrender control of all of European Turkey except Istanbul. Izmir was to be placed under Greek administration pending a plebiscite. Italy, France and Britain were each to have a "zone of influence" in southern Anatolia. An independent Armenia was to be created near the Russian border; the Kurds were promised an autonomous Kurdistan. The Dardanelles was to be put under international control. Turkey's economy was to be placed under Allied direction and its Army reduced to a token force.

THE terms accepted by the Sultan's Government gave Atatürk's nationalists an immense advantage. The entire nation, however much involved with the Sultan's Government, however much conditioned to loyalty to the Ottoman dynasty, became emotionally involved with Atatürk's increasingly successful resistance to the invaders. The despised Greeks drove deep into the country, but they found the subjugation of western Anatolia impossible in the face of resistance by Atatürk's forces. As Turkish successes grew—eventually the Greeks were driven back to Izmir—Britain, France and Italy, emotionally less committed than the Greeks, withdrew their forces after only token resistance. In 1923 a peace treaty was signed in Switzerland which recognized that Anatolia had been cleared of foreign control.

Having as commander in chief of the victorious armies plotted the war of Turkish survival, Atatürk now insisted on the right to plot the route of Turkish revolution. With a mixture of inspiring leadership and political ruthlessness he presented his country not with a committee of conflicting idealists but with one stern physician: himself. The patient, Turkey, was to submit to his diagnosis; the diagnosis made, he, and no one else, would provide the cure.

ATATURK'S diagnosis was radical and simple. Turkey's ailments, he felt, derived in part from historical accident: through their conversion to Islam the Turks over the centuries had become chained to a backward Eastern society marked by ignorance, illiteracy and bigotry. The redemption of the Turkish destiny was possible, Atatürk believed, only if the Turks broke with the East and created a modern Turkish state, which would take its place with the other modern states of Europe.

The diagnosis had been fitfully prepared over four decades of a man's life. In Salonika Atatürk had seen that the polyglot Ottoman Empire did not command the allegiance of the non-Turkish, non-Moslem millets. In the Arab provinces he had seen that the empire, despite its pretensions to the leadership of world Islam, had lost the affection of the Moslem Arabs. In war he had realized that the Turkish Army, drawn from the Anatolian peasantry, had fought unending battles for this unviable empire. In Istanbul he had seen that the leadership of the empire esteemed the *efendi,* the smooth cosmopolitan, not the brave if uncouth *köylü,* or villager, who did the actual fighting for the empire. In Sofia he had first been dazzled by the appeal of Western civilization. In the holy Arab city of Damascus he had drawn the conclusion that it was the Moslem religion that gave the city its atmosphere of repression and bigotry. It was Islam, he felt, that had prevented the peoples of the Ottoman Empire from developing in the enlightened ways of the West.

The diagnosis made, the physician proceeded, with the utmost skill and considerable dissimulation, to present his countrymen with a cure in several stages.

First, the schism between the Sultan's Government in Istanbul and his own Government in Ankara—the Sultan's discredited by defeat and subservience, Atatürk's free and victorious—gave Atatürk his opportunity to abolish the sultanate. In the autumn of 1922 Mehmet VI, the last Sultan of the Ottoman house, fled his palace and boarded a British warship for the safety of Malta and eventual death in exile. A year after his departure the Grand National Assembly proclaimed a Turkish republic and elected Atatürk its first President. The choice of Ankara as the capital of the new republic, rather than imperial Istanbul, symbolically destroyed the concept of a territorial power ruling various nations in one great empire. In its place, and inside the frontiers that defeat (and limited victory) had left, the Turkish republic was to safeguard the destiny of the Anatolian Turks.

To offset conservative opposition to the abolition of the sultanate Atatürk thought it temporarily advisable to preserve the religious functions the Sultan had exercised in his role as Caliph. Mehmet's cousin Abdül Mecid, a gentle, scholarly man, was appointed Caliph. Some theorists argued that this arrangement could be a permanent one. The president would represent the secular power, the caliph the spiritual. But Atatürk was not attracted by such a solution on a long-term basis. In the past the entrenched forces of Islamic orthodoxy, with the caliph at their head, had more than once blocked the efforts of reformers. In March 1924 the caliphate was abolished.

WITH this act the link between Turkey and world Islam was snapped. Subsequent events confirmed the break. At home the Ministry of Religious Laws and Pious Foundations was abolished. Religious seminaries were closed down. The dervish orders, which had contributed a warmth otherwise lacking in the legalistic fabric of Turkish Islam, were outlawed. Shrines that had been focuses of religious life and pilgrimage were proscribed as places of worship. The religious courts that still applied the holy law of the Koran in matters like marriages, divorce and inheritance were abolished. To replace the holy law the Civil Code of Switzerland was taken over almost completely intact.

These measures against the institutions of Islam were not criticized in the West, where Islam was little understood and less valued. But in Turkey the acts aroused resistance and left grave problems for the future. Atatürk's prestige was so great, in a nation where military success and religion had long gone together, that his subjects' favorite name for him was *"Gazi,"* the traditional Islamic title for a warrior against the infidel. It had been granted him by the Turkish parliament after his victory over the Greeks. But his measures against Islam—inspired by resentment of clerical interference in politics—were disliked and after his death were to be contested.

OF all Atatürk's reforms the one that generated the greatest resentment was the abolition of the fez. Introduced only a century before, the fez had taken on a deep significance for Turkish Moslems. It had become a mark of their loyalty to Islam and of their rejection of other faiths. As the British scholar G. L. Lewis had pointed out, even the Turkish word for hat—*şapka*—had acquired unpleasant connotations. The words *"şapka giymek"*—"to put on a hat"—implied a desertion of Islam or even entry into the service of a foreign power. But Atatürk became the hat's champion. In a speech in one of the most conservative regions of Anatolia he once said: "A civilized, international dress is worthy and appropriate for our nation, and we will wear it. Boots or shoes on our feet, trousers on our legs, shirt and tie, jacket and waistcoat—and of course, to complete these, a cover with a brim on our heads. I wish to say this openly. The name of this head covering is 'hat.'"

In other matters affecting the personal lives of the Turks, Atatürk was also a revolutionary. He fought for the emancipation of women. In so doing he could claim to be going back to Turkish tradition. Whatever the origin of the harem system, it was not Turkish. In Central Asia Turkish queens had been as important as Turkish kings. But as Byzantine and Persian influences took hold, Ottoman women became almost totally segregated. The custom of veiling the face was universal; women were regarded as playthings, prized when playful, relegated to the role of servants or slaves when their beauty had withered.

The decline of the Ottoman Empire had coincided with the birth of women's hopes to play a larger

share in society, and the war of Turkish survival finally gave women their chance. Halide Edib, the impassioned graduate of the American Girls College
who had attempted to rouse resistance in Istanbul
at the outset of the war, became a sergeant in the
Army; humbler women helped to carry arms to the
front by hand or bullock cart. In 1921 Ismail Hakkı
Baltacıoğlu, head of the Faculty of Arts at Istanbul
University, agreed to allow women to attend lectures
with men. But it was Atatürk's admirable persistence
that resulted in the total abolition of the legal restrictions placed on women. Under the terms of the
Swiss Civil Code adopted in 1926, polygamy was
outlawed, women received the right to initiate divorce proceedings, and the inheritance laws were
changed to give women equal rights with men. In
1930 women were allowed to vote in municipal elections, and four years later they were given the right
to vote in national elections and to be elected to
parliament.

IF Turkish women had become shrouded in non-
Turkish veils, so in Atatürk's opinion had the
Turkish language. The warrior-nomads from Central
Asia had spoken one of the world's great languages,
different in structure from both the Indo-European
family of tongues spoken in Europe, India and Persia and the Semitic languages of the Middle East and
Africa. The Turkish language was kept muscular by
poetry and musical by a sense for euphony that was
more highly developed, perhaps, than in any other
language.

When the Ottoman Empire was established, Turkish became its language. The language that the
Turks had brought from Central Asia had, however,
become overlaid with borrowings from Persian and
Arabic. It was not simply that Turkish had borrowed as many conceptual words from these two
more sophisticated tongues as English has taken
from Latin and Greek. It was that Turkish gram-
mar had often been forced into alien molds. To
understand Ottoman Turkish a man had to know,
for example, not only the Turkish method of form-
ing plurals (by adding -*ler* or -*lar* to the noun) but
also the Arabic and Persian methods. Thus the Arabic
loan word *"kitap,"* or *"book,"* had its plural formed
on Arabic lines and became *"kutup."*

So much for the words themselves. The Arabic
letters in which they came to be written were even
more constricting. Arabic is a language uncommon-
ly rich in consonants but poor in vowels; the re-
verse is true of Turkish. And yet, by the historical
accident of Islamization, Turkish was expressing itself in an alphabet that was complicated and ill-
adapted to its use.

That Atatürk was right in his desire to reform both
language and alphabet is hardly open to question.
Ottoman Turkish had become a mandarin tongue
that was very far from intelligible to the ordinary
Turk. He embarked on his linguistic reforms with
his usual energy. He formed an Alphabet Commission in 1928. Told that expert opinion advocated a
five-year transition period, during which the old Arabic and the proposed new Latin scripts would co-
exist, Atatürk insisted that "the change will happen
in three months or it will not happen at all." Within
six weeks the commission had prepared a new alphabet. On August 9 Atatürk himself demonstrated the
new letters on a blackboard at an open-air meeting
in Istanbul, and within the allotted three months
the Turkish parliament had passed legislation adopt-
ing the new alphabet and prohibiting the use of the
Arabic alphabet after the end of the year. The alphabet was a success; it has stood the test of time and
has greatly facilitated an increase in literacy.

ATATURK also endorsed a rigorous pruning of
"non-Turkish" elements in the language, and
the chief victims were words borrowed from Arabic,
which had provided a large proportion of the Ottoman Turkish vocabulary. Critics could argue that it
was not a word's derivation from outside that often
irritated Atatürk, but the derivation from Arabic.
Words derived from French or Italian were happily
substituted for words derived from Arabic. At the
same time pedants ransacked archaic Turkish texts
and tribal dialects to find new Turkish words for
Arabic words that had become completely assimilat-
ed. These new Turkish words were often completely
unintelligible to the people who were supposed to
use them. The possibility arose that not only would
the new generation encounter difficulty in reading
the literature of the past, but the "Turkification"
of the language might make Atatürk's own sayings

unintelligible to future generations. Atatürk's famous six-day speech, for example, which was delivered in 1927, is today a difficult and archaic text for schoolchildren, and they can grasp its meaning only through reliance on a multitude of footnotes and explanations. Inevitably the attempt at language reform caused difficulties and aroused general irritation among the people.

In the 1930s Atatürk was taken in by a crackpot theory put forward by a Viennese philologist which seemed to offer a way out. This "Sun Language" theory claimed that primitive man had uttered his first words in an expression of awe at the sight of the sun. These words could not be linked to Indo-European or Semitic roots, but the scholar had found that they might be linked to Turkish, and thus Turkish could well be the "mother of all languages." Atatürk at once ordered this theory taught at the newly founded Faculty of Letters in Ankara. To Turkish language reformers, the theory had the virtue of justifying the retention of many Arabic, Persian and Latin words—since all the languages in the world had sprung originally from Turkish. Although this proposition was soon discredited by more reliable scholars, forcing Atatürk himself to back away from it, its temporary adoption at least helped put a brake on too precipitous a dismantling of the spoken tongue.

Abolition of sultanate and caliphate, dress and language reform, even the formal emancipation of women—such things could be achieved by legislation. Profounder reforms—such as the over-all development of Anatolia, the modernization of agriculture and mass education—were four-dimensional, stretching into the future. These would, in their success and failure, form the history of modern Turkey, and they are treated in later chapters in this book. They were part of the over-all struggle to raise the Turks to a material level comparable to that enjoyed by the people of the West.

THE broad lines of what had to be done were, however, clearly pointed out by Atatürk. By his oft-quoted statement that "the *efendi* of our nation is the villager," he implied that the values of centuries had to be transformed. The villager, Atatürk believed, must demonstrate the confidence of,

and receive the respect of, the Ottoman *efendi*. To acquire this confidence, to win this respect, he had to be educated. Schools had to be brought to the villages. Adults had to be trained to new tasks.

To these goals Atatürk could only point. History and the geography of Anatolia dictated that the journey would take decades.

INDUSTRIAL development also needed time. In 1923, the year of the proclamation of the republic, the Turkish industrial plant had been about as rudimentary as Atatürk's ideas of economics. The formula adopted in 1931—which came to be called etatism, massive state participation in the starting and managing of basic industries—was to create the morass of bureaucracy and inefficiency that has formed around so many socialist projects. Yet in the hopeful dawn of the new Turkey, etatism seemed an effective way to create industries that the country needed. Encouraged to reject the tradition that trade was undignified, Turkish Moslems plunged, often ineptly, into business. Turkey's economic progress during Atatürk's life was to be considerable but scarcely sufficient to the nation's needs.

Atatürk also left the development of political democracy to the future. His own temperament became increasingly autocratic; as early as 1920 his frank insistence that everyone should obey him absolutely shocked such outspoken idealists as Halide Edib; she predicted that while Atatürk alone had the energy to win the war of survival, his revolution would allow little room for liberal principles. She foresaw rightly. But the remarkable thing about Atatürk, autocrat that he was, was his insistence that Turkey should eventually become a democracy, even if during his own lifetime he felt that opposition parties were a luxury and a danger that the fledgling republic could not risk. With clear-sightedness and logic Atatürk had recognized that much of the West's dynamism derived not from machine guns or particular styles of clothing but from political freedom. At a time when some Western countries were turning to dictatorship it would have been easy for Atatürk to have rationalized his own control of power into a theory. He did not. He saw that if Turkey were to progress in a Western manner, it must do so as a democratic state.

EFFECTIVE ORATOR, Mustafa Kemal in 1923 addresses a crowd in southern Turkey. In the preceding four years the magnetic leader had defeated an invading Greek army and had secured control over much of the territory of Anatolia, which the victorious Allies had planned to dispose of after World War I. Later in 1923 he became President of the new Turkish republic.

PROMISING OFFICER, Colonel Mustafa Kemal *(second from left)* is photographed in 1915. Colonel Kemal was soon to play a major role in the defeat of Allied forces at Gallipoli.

A Complex and Extraordinary Leader

Given the name Kemal, or "Perfection," by a schoolmaster, the boy known originally only as Mustafa was as a man surnamed Atatürk—"Father Turk"—by his country's assembly. The superlatives conceal Atatürk's contradictions. There is no argument that he was an able, even a brilliant, soldier. It is also indisputable that he was a visionary statesman. Atatürk urged on Turkey an enlightened program of universal education, adoption of the Latin alphabet, equal rights for women and industrialization. He tried to break the power of Moslem leaders out of touch with the times; by the scruff of the neck he tried to haul his nation into the 20th Century. Yet while insisting on democratic forms he autocratically dictated the country's course. Today Turkey, still creeping toward his goals, has forgotten most of the bad and remembers all of the good of Father Turk.

STRONG-WILLED PRESIDENT, Atatürk issues an order *(right)* in 1936. Although he maintained the forms of democracy, his party's candidates often ran for office unopposed.

ATATURK'S MEMORY, nurtured by monuments and memorials, is a part of the national consciousness

BEFORE A PARADE honoring Atatürk, two soldiers keep guard near an Ankara monument that also honors him. The circles *(foreground)* mark places assigned to parade reviewers.

INSIDE THE MAUSOLEUM in Ankara where Atatürk is buried, former Prime Minister Ismet Inönü *(center)* and other Turkish dignitaries hear tribute paid to their onetime leader.

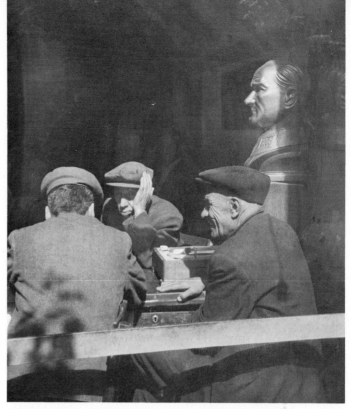

UNDER A BUST of Atatürk, men of the town of Afyon while away the weekend in a café. Near Afyon, Atatürk's troops captured the commander of disorganized Greek invaders in 1922.

IN A SMALL TOWN, plaster heads of Atatürk are delivered by wagon to their destinations *(below)*. Public places throughout Turkey display effigies of the country's founding father.

*BUSY ANKARA, designated
the country's capital by Atatürk
in 1923, is the most
Westernized city in Turkey*

HURRIED CITIZENS stride along a thoroughfare in Ankara. Once a sleepy provincial town, Ankara is now a bustling capital of administrators and military officers.

ATATURK BOULEVARD courses past modern office buildings *(left)*. The city was built on a European-style plan, with radiating boulevards and many spacious parks.

PROUD FATHER shows his child to acquaintances. Most of the people of Ankara were born elsewhere. The rapid population expansion has caused some slum growth.

ELEGANT AUDIENCE chats at the National Opera House *(right)*. Ankara's citizens enjoy Western music, but most of the Turks still prefer traditional styles.

YOUNG BUSINESSMEN converse in a café *(below)*. The choice of Ankara as the capital, rather than Istanbul, was intended as a symbolic break with the Ottoman past.

A peasant of an eastern village sits at home with his five children. In the corner one of the women of the family modestly hides beh

84

so that a stranger—the photographer—will not see her face.

6

The Anatolian Homeland

THE Turkish homeland of Anatolia was the arena where the revolutionary theories proposed by Atatürk (see Chapter 5) had to be made fact. This upland area of plateau and plain, forest and valley, great lakes and mountains—and of primitive villages wedded to a traditional way of life —presented a redoubtable challenge to even so formidable a remaker of a society. Today change is at last reshaping Anatolia.

Nowhere can the effort to respond to the challenge posed by Atatürk be better observed than in Ankara, the Anatolian city chosen as the capital of the new Turkish republic in 1923. Atatürk had selected Ankara because of the friendly feeling of its citizens toward his movement. A negative reason was its utter unlikeness to sophisticated Istanbul, where a time bomb set by the Byzantines (it may have seemed to Atatürk) had ticked on and on until it exploded, bringing ruin to the Ottomans, who long ago had captured the city from them with such pride.

Ankara's growth has been remarkable. In 1923, when the national assembly passed a special law setting forth its plans for the development of the town, Ankara had a population of 27,000 persons. When the most recent census was taken, in 1960, it had a population of 680,000. By 1965 the city contained an estimated 800,000 people.

A visitor may approach Ankara from either the West or the East. The direction from which he comes will make a great difference in his reactions. If he flies to Anatolia from the West, Ankara's boulevards and grayish, 1930s-style architecture may remind him of a suburb of Berlin. The slightly Teutonic atmosphere probably derives from the activities of Hermann Jansen, a German city planner who was Ankara's architectural director some 30 years ago. There is a preponderance of bulky banks whose names light up at night: Sugar Bank, Sumerian Bank, Hittite Bank. The National Theater, with its drab pillars, resembles other functional theaters put up in the 1930s and 1940s. Atatürk Bulvari, the great boulevard which forms the vertebral column of the city, is lined with architecturally undistinguished colleges, institutes and shops, and modest, three-story buildings. To a Westerner paying his pennies to enter the Youth Park, cafés, cabarets and an artificial lake bring a yawn of recognition: they are the standard amusements in a municipal background.

THE visitor from the West may, therefore, discover the old city with relief. He will find a citadel which was in existence long before the Mongol conqueror Tamerlane attacked it in the 15th Century, a citadel old when the Roman Emperor Augustus ordered his autobiography inscribed on the portico of one of the city's temples or when St. Paul wrote his Epistle to the inhabitants of the time, the Galatians.

Someone coming to Ankara from the East will have a more positive reaction than a visitor reaching it from the West. He will be impressed by the contrast between Ankara's clean, wide streets, orderly traffic, tree-freshened sidewalks and the rabbit-warren alleys of the hamlets of the East. So much of the East, in Turkey as well as in its neighbors Iran and Iraq, carries an oppressive burden of ossified traditions that it becomes exciting to find in the middle of Anatolia a city that is basically modern

and new. The very existence of a theater at which *Op Beni, Kate (Kiss Me, Kate)* can be seen is a delight.

It is this aspect of Ankara that the people of Anatolia prefer to see. Because of the attraction of this big, Western-style city, squatters have covered the surrounding hills with shacks which the Turks call *gecekondu,* or "built by night."

EVEN in its difficulties Ankara is a modern, developing city, pioneer in an East that had been for a long time stagnant. City officials discuss their problems with the frankness of elected officials in a free society. Halil Sezai Erkut, who became the Mayor of Ankara in 1964, is a graduate of the Ankara University law school. He is representative of the best kind of new Turk—animated, energetic and sincere. He is willing to admit, for example, that 300,000 squatters live in the fly-by-night shacks. Erkut is of the West in his confidence that such problems should be solved, not ignored. Soon after moving into the mayor's office he brought electricity to almost all of the city's slum areas and laid 60 miles of water pipelines. But he foresaw graver problems, problems which citizens of big cities in other countries will recognize.

Ankara's population may double in another generation. Water will then be a severe problem. Ankara's water now comes from the Cubuk River, which is only a short distance away; in the future, other, more distant sources will have to be tapped. Additional electric power will also have to come from afar. One of the major sources presently in use lies 185 miles away at Catalağzı, near the great coal port of Zonguldak on the Black Sea. Another problem is the lack of an adequate sewage system. Although traffic is only beginning to be troublesome Ankara already shares an affliction with Los Angeles. Smog from cheap lignite coal makes winter days malodorous in the bowl of hills in which Ankara sits.

This is a formidable list of problems. But there is something about Ankara that is zestful and optimistic. The young men and women who throng the sidewalks have a spring in their step which is not noticeable in shuffling Istanbul. The cafés under the chestnut trees are crowded; talk is, if not raucous, at least lively. Laughter is not unknown.

If Ankara is the prime example of modernized Anatolia, this is not to say that there are no others, or that they are all modernizing in the same way. Adana in the fertile Cukurova plain is an ugly but prosperous boomtown. There industry and commerce, bursting the bonds of a decorous past, have created a jerry-built but vital city where the huge American cars of newly rich cotton kings block the narrow, one-way streets. Zonguldak, Samsun and Trabzon, all cities on the Black Sea coast, have developed rapidly in recent years, thanks to such products as coal, tobacco and corn. Izmir on the Aegean has continued to export the fruits which grow so prodigiously in the fertile valleys along the coast and which made the fortunes of Greek settlers of former times.

A PLACE in which Atatürk's effort to transform Anatolia by establishing state industries can be observed is Kırıkkale, a city lying in rugged, empty highlands 50 miles northeast of Ankara. Kırıkkale was less than a hamlet in 1928 when Atatürk started an arms factory there as one of his state enterprises. Kırıkkale is now a pleasant place of pink-washed villas with red tile roofs. Its population, swollen to about 50,000, seems proud that Kırıkkale's six Government-owned factories now supply some small arms and ammunition to Germany, since the original machinery came from Germany almost 40 years ago—although Salem, Ohio, is written on later additions to the plant.

Recep Teoman, a graduate of the Technical University of Istanbul, has grown with the town. When he was a boy, Teoman recalls, Kırıkkale was small and dull. "My friends and I had little to do but watch the train from Iraq go through. Once we heard that the most beautiful girl in Baghdad would be traveling. It was lonely, but we waited hours. We were disappointed, however. The only female we could see was a wretched old hag."

Teoman is director of Kırıkkale's copper and brass plant. In his domain, a vast hall where stubborn earth is turned into tubes and gaskets, there is something more revolutionary than the machines: a small, blue box fixed to one wall and labeled *Teklif Kutusu*, or Suggestion Box. Instead of a traditional insistence

upon obedience, this portion of modern Turkey encourages complaints, criticisms and new ideas—all of which are freely ventilated at weekly meetings between management and labor.

Ankara and the other Anatolian centers of modernity, although growing in number and quality, strikingly contrast with their own hinterland. The dominant element in the hinterland, the true Anatolian, is the *köylü*, or villager. It is doubtful that he has even begun to feel himself what Atatürk wished him to be: "the *efendi* of Turkey." The cities, with their higher standard of living, remain the preserve of those who are successful, and between them and the villages there remains an abyss. Not that the men and women of the cities are hostile to the villages; on the contrary, they wish them well. But their benevolence is often remote, like the benevolence of the wellborn women in the West who used to patronize soup kitchens for the deserving poor. The poverty of Anatolia, and what to do about it, is a favorite topic of urban conversation. An Istanbul feminist, for example, who supplements her income by selling her own modern paintings, asked rhetorically not long ago: "What is wrong with Anatolia? The peasant husbands! The lazy Anatolians would like to keep our women as dray horses. We should go to the villages and arouse the women." Another woman later commented sadly: "Can you imagine these lacquered clubwomen agitating our farmers' wives?" The picture is unimaginable. Its impossibility underlines the schism between educated and uneducated which President Cemal Gürsel has defined as the major difficulty of modern Turkey.

A LTHOUGH the republic has been in existence for more than 40 years, Government figures show that at least 60 per cent of the Anatolians are still illiterate—a figure comparable to that of Egypt, another Middle Eastern country whose population is approximately the same as Turkey's, but whose revolution did not take place until 1952. Those who know the Anatolians agree that the villagers have a longfelt prejudice against government, whatever the nature of that government. There is a traditional fear of showing wealth when wealth exists, for to those living in the country, the city seems the enemy, not the big brother. From the point of view of the *köylü*, the government official's purpose in contacting him is likely to be unpleasant—the collection of taxes or interference with cherished customs.

Turkish villages do not resemble those of Europe; nor is the setting of Turkish rural life entirely similar to that of Egypt. While Egypt's 28 million people live in one long, warm valley linked by one river, one road and one railway, Anatolia's 35,000 villages are separated by an obstinate geography and are subjected, in many regions, to a ruthless climate. While an Arab villager's poverty is often offset by sunshine, a villager in central or eastern Anatolia looks toward each dour winter with something akin to dread. The great fear is whether the villagers' stores of food will last through to the next harvest. The food reserves are often kept in large holes in front of the village houses. When it rains—and this is the country where Noah's ark floated finally to rest on flood-surmounting Ararat—the peasants have to squat over their stores to prevent them from being ruined.

Inside the houses, heat is provided by the *tandır*, another hole in the earth. Except in forested areas the fuel burned in the *tandır* is dry buffalo dung. The heat is retained by a table-shaped platform above the hole; over this is stretched a *kilim*, or rug, often in the vivid colors which have made the peasant carpets prized purchases for visitors to Turkey's markets. At night mattresses are laid around the *tandır;* eight or more people will sleep with their feet toward the warmth.

THE backwardness of village life has been an extraordinarily difficult problem to deal with—and the solution to the problem defied both Atatürk and his successor, Ismet Inönü. Nor was much done under either man to diminish the distrust between town and country. While Atatürk and his aides were preoccupied with the cultural revolution, foreign affairs and the starting of industry, a new group, the *ağas*, began to dominate much of the countryside. Unlike the Ottoman beys whom they replaced, and who had retained some of the humane values of a traditional culture, the *ağas* were newly rich peasants who had profiteered in the chaotic years following World War I. The original meaning of *ağa* was "master" or "older person"; it acquired a new,

despotic meaning for many Turks. In a number of areas the *ağas* became the effective means of contact between rulers and ruled: the peasant wanting something from the Government worked through his *ağa*, while the Government used the *ağa* when it wanted votes or taxes.

YASAR KEMAL, a writer who was born among the peasantry, has indicated this *ağa* class with informed precision. Kemal's novel *Memed, My Hawk* is set in one particular locality—the Cukurova—but many of its insights into peasant life are true of Anatolia in general. Slim Memed, the hero, is an orphan who, cheated out of his land, becomes a brigand. On the symbolic level, he represents the conscience of the tyrannized villagers. There is something angelic about this Turkish Robin Hood: a strange, yellow light, Kemal relates, suffuses and illuminates him in the moment when he decides on right action. The villagers are shown as docile, vacillating and harassed. They can do nothing for themselves. They need a hawk, an angel, to avenge them against an *ağa* to whom they cannot help being servile. The chief *ağa*, the Sheriff of Nottingham of this naïve but powerful tale, is called Ali Safa Bey. Himself the son of a dispossessed *ağa*, he regains his father's land by using legal quibbles against the villagers. Playing one village against another, he acquires half the land of both villages. When finally resisted he unleashes brigands against those who oppose him. As a result his land doubles in a few years. While Memed the Hawk eventually kills the *ağa* of his own village, the chief *ağa*, Ali Safa Bey, is still pursuing his predatory ways at the novel's end.

This portrayal of the peasants is confirmed by Richard D. Robinson, a Harvard specialist in Turkish history who spent several years in central Anatolia. In a typical village, he has remarked, "The only property held in common is the mosque, the cemetery, the village spring, and a crude stone bath. There is no communal road-building activity (although the village roads are in sad shape), no communally owned crop land, no collectively owned agricultural equipment, no marketing or consumers' cooperatives, no community effort to beautify the village or improve its sanitation, no organization for improving or cleaning village streets. There is no collective enterprise to speak of except that dictated by sheer necessity."

When Atatürk pointed the way to the development of Anatolia he believed that the villages could be converted to an acceptance of modern values by lay missionaries, the secular schoolteachers. In an early move toward achieving mass literacy, Army sergeants were given short courses and then sent to teach the rudiments of reading and writing in their villages. This interest in the education of the villagers reached a further stage in 1940 when Ismail Hakkı Tonguç, the country's brilliant Director of Primary Education, began to establish a number of schools called Village Institutes throughout Turkey, with the cooperation of the Minister of Education, Hasan Ali Yücel. Tonguç had become aware that the Anatolians needed something more than mere academic instruction: they needed to acquire a vigorous sense of self-help as well, and to master simple skills which could help to raise the level of village existence. In the Institutes the students—selected from the villages—spent half their time in lessons, half in practical work. After a short period the students acquired a useful smattering of a wide range of techniques—the rudiments of weaving, farming, handicrafts, even medicine—and were sent back to their villages.

A young graduate of one of these Institutes, Mahmut Makal, has written perhaps the most moving and realistic description ever made of an Anatolian peasant community in a book that he called, simply, *Our Village*. Makal was born in the village of Demirci, near Aksaray in central Anatolia, in 1930. Although his experiences as a 17-year-old teacher were in an area which was perhaps more wretched than some zones of Turkey, and although his description of these experiences was written some years ago, *Our Village* remains a key to understanding the continuing crisis of Anatolia. As the British

A NAME FOR TURKEYS AND TURKS

The word "turkey" has held a variety of meanings. To the Pilgrims, the large fowl they encountered resembled a bird that Turkish merchants had been importing into Europe and that had come to be known as a "turkey." The word itself possibly derived from *T'u-chueh,* the name given by the Chinese to the ancestors of the modern Turks. "Turk" was used by Europeans to designate a subject of the Ottoman Empire; in the empire itself, however, it came to mean a barbarian. It was not until the Atatürk revolution that the Turks, searching for a new, non-Ottoman identity, adopted "Turks" and "Turkey."

anthropologist Paul Stirling has written: "Mahmut Makal is the first genuine villager, from the inarticulate millions of peasants all over the world, to describe the village from within." The impact of Makal's sketches, when they were published in the review *Varlık,* was so great that for a while he was imprisoned and the name of his village was changed.

The hostility was understandable. Makal's study of village life is no pastoral idyl. What emerges is the triviality and lack of satisfaction of village life. The people are underfed and bored.

"It's winter," Makal writes. "It's not done for a man to stay at home. He gets up at dawn, throws a little straw to his beasts, provides himself with several loaves of bread, slips on his clogs, and makes for the village room. Everyone who can conceivably be called a man is there, even little boys on their grandfathers' knees. The families of the village have each given a measure of rye to buy the stove, which draws badly, so the room is always full of smoke. A charming place, where one can neither hear nor see. I go there only seldom. Someone spots me. 'You're leaving? Perhaps you fear lice?' I am leaving because I have work to do. But if you ask me the truth about the lice, the fleas, the dust, ah well! Even the precious DDT can't do much.

"Even before sunrise the room is full to bursting. It is at this hour that one can see the loaves of bread spread around the stove like laundry drying. The men . . . eat them as breakfast on their knees. After that things start: they begin to play at knucklebones. . . . A big circle forms. Those who withdraw are at once replaced. It will be like this until evening; sometimes until next morning. Each player opens a pack of cigarettes. . . . He will remain kneeling ten hours, twenty hours. He will win two cigarettes, or lose four. What counts is to kill time."

Some houses do not have indoor toilets. The members of the family relieve themselves just outside the door. Fowl scratch the ground and a filthy dust blows indoors. When Makal, apostle of simple enlightenment, complains, a householder says: "I agree, it would be better to go farther away. But you see, none of us has shoes; in cold weather it would be too far to go."

The *hoja,* or village clergyman, has a clock, but he encourages no one to consult it. The time of day is based on the times of prayer. There is a stone in front of the mosque. When the sun reaches it, it is time for midday prayer. A shadow crosses the road —it is time for afternoon prayer. When the sun reddens the horizon it is time for evening prayer. Otherwise no one thinks of time.

Makal vividly illustrates the problem of illiteracy. He encounters a poor old man riding, in the middle of the night, toward the distant town. The Government has sent him an official summons. No one in the village can read it, not even the boys recently back from military service. The *muhtar,* or headman, himself illiterate, has pretended that the letter requires the old man's immediate presence in court. Makal tells the old man that the appointment is in fact for the following week.

The immense distances of Anatolia were long an obstacle to those few peasants who dreamed of rising above subsistence level. A story is told of two men who collect 100 turkeys with the idea of selling them at the best possible price. "Let's go to Ankara," one suggests. "There turkeys fetch fantastic prices." They load a donkey with maize and set off. They walk and walk. Where is Ankara? Fifty-five days later they come back. All is lost. Their turkeys were walked to the bone. Some of them were stolen. The story quickly becomes a proverb of folly: "Go to Ankara to sell turkeys."

Women do most of the heavy work. They look after the animals, fetch water for the house. "Yet

their prestige," Makal reports, "is diametrically opposite to that of their sisters in the cities. Women as such have no value except in the first days of marriage. Slaves and servants, they make no decisions. The man can stretch himself on his bed and say: 'Woman, do this, do that.' She will never dare say, 'Let's do so and so.' A woman is valued by the respect she shows for her husband. A husband can manhandle her, she must never protest. Her pride is to obey her husband in detail. His right is to punish her without appeal. There is no idea of life companionship."

"Respect for the beard" dictates that if a woman is 200 paces ahead of a man, she will wait until he has caught up with her, even if she is heavily burdened. A village saying goes: "Evil be to her who overtakes a man."

At first reading, Makal's portrait is somber. What relieves the gloom is not merely the reflection that it is no longer strictly up to date, but the evidence it gives of the energy and dedication of men like Makal himself. Anatolian sloth can hardly help but give way before their efforts. The young Makal was naturally depressed by his own failure to make much immediate impact. The villagers still seemed to prefer wandering preachers and storytellers to himself and his young colleagues with their newer wares.

The educational effort of which Makal was a part has continued to develop. In 1954 the Democrat Party reorganized the Institutes into regular teacher-training institutions on the grounds that they were separating the villages from the cities and incidentally giving rise to Communist ideas. But the basic ideals of the Institutes persist.

The original Institute is located at Hasanoğlan, 20 miles east of Ankara. Nazım Esen, a burly, middle-aged man of great gentleness, slow speech and evident kindness, became director of the institution,

---

THE KORAN ON WOMAN'S ROLE

The subservient role long assigned to women in much of the Islamic world has a justification in the Koran—the revealed word of Allah as spoken by his prophet, Mohammed.

Men are the managers of the affairs of women for that God has preferred in bounty one of them over another, and for that they have expended of their property. Righteous women are therefore obedient, guarding the secret for God's guarding. And those you fear may be rebellious admonish; banish them to their couches, and beat them. If they then obey you, look not for any way against them; God is All-high, All-great.
And if you fear a breach between the two, bring forth an arbiter from his people and from her people an arbiter, if they desire to set things right; God will compose their differences; surely God is All-knowing, All-aware.

now known as the Atatürk Primary Teachers' School, in 1961. As such he presided over a vast campus of buildings, including an open-air theater which holds 10,000 people. For a period of six years Hasanoğlan is home for more than 1,200 children, almost one third of them girls.

Among Hasanoğlan's 48 teachers is Ahmet Kayalıdere. Slight, dark and enthusiastic, he specializes in English and music. Since music will be part of the curriculum in the villages, the campus is crowded on sunny afternoons with boys and girls strumming on the *saz*, a mandolinlike instrument. Kayalıdere, himself a villager from Polatlı, was a student at Hasanoğlan in its opening days. He proudly displays a gallery of photographs illustrating the school's history. Some of them show boys in Anatolian village costume, ragged rather than picturesque, mixing concrete and carrying bricks in 1941 as foundations for the first buildings were laid on land belonging to the state. The school attracted few students in those days; now every year only 200 out of 4,000 applicants can be accepted. It is probably no exaggeration to say that the real work of modernizing Turkey is being done by men such as Nazım Esen, Ahmet Kayalıdere and their colleagues in the other teacher-training schools scattered around the country.

OF all the areas of Anatolia the region east of the Euphrates has been the most neglected. Here travel by foreigners was forbidden for many years; the prohibition may have been due quite as much to embarrassment at foreign observation of backwardness as to fear of espionage in an area so close to the Russian border.

The Village Institutes constituted an attack on the basic problems presented by the backwardness of the rural areas. Atatürk University, which was established in 1958 at Erzurum, the major city of eastern Anatolia, represented the beginning of an attack on the problem of development at a higher level. Like many universities in the Middle East and Asia, the formal, older universities of Ankara and Istanbul are not only desperately overcrowded (there are almost 2,000 first-year students enrolled in Istanbul's law school), but are remote from the villagers' practical needs. They tend to perpetuate and enlarge a professional class with privileged standards of living rather than to produce pioneers willing to work in the eastern provinces. The ratio of doctors per head in Istanbul is, for example, 65 times higher than the ratio in the eastern provinces.

ATATURK UNIVERSITY differs from the classical universities of Ankara and Istanbul in its functionalism: its courses are designed to be directly related to the pressing needs of the Anatolian villages. Significantly, it is affiliated with the University of Nebraska, which possesses one of the United States' major agricultural-research departments. American advisers and teachers are particularly active in the largest department, agriculture. An imposing hostel houses and feeds students from remote Van or Artvin, on the Russian border, for as little as $15 a month. Many students are on scholarship and pay nothing at all.

Once the home of Midas, the Phrygian King at whose touch dross turned to gold, Anatolia is potentially rich. At present it is extremely poor. The gap between what it is now and what it could be often causes either bitter despair or bitter resentment. To bridge the gap will take time, although purveyors of panaceas, both extreme nationalist and extreme Leftist, busily if surreptitiously hawk their wares. Turkey's rulers realize the importance of capital development and the need for engineers. Good communications can make market outlets more accessible, enabling future peasants to sell their turkeys at a profit. During the 15 years since Mahmut Makal described his Anatolian village, there has been a spectacular improvement in Turkish communications. Turkey now has some 38,000 miles of national and provincial roads, of which roughly 16,000 are state highways. The U.S. has made major contributions to the building of this highway system.

Educated Turks know that in the past Anatolia supported great civilizations, but they are aware that the alchemy of Midas is not what is needed. The transformation of Anatolia must start in the minds and hearts of its men and women. There are no short cuts. The heroes of this long and arduous road are the teachers. The children at Hasanoğlan have a seriousness, even a solemnity, of manner which shows their awareness of their future role.

MOUNTAIN TOWN not far from Ankara slumbers through the harsh winter under a mantle of snow. The region has fertile soil capable of producing a variety of crops, but aridity is a constant problem on the central plateau and seven out of the 12 months of the year are likely to be rainless.

WATER RATION is collected in buckets *(below)* from the well of a small village in eastern Turkey. Grains like wheat and barley are grown here. Rainfall is seriously erratic, but eastern Turkey receives more rain than does the central plateau —averaging between 17 and 24 inches annually.

Along a snow-covered lane near Van in eastern Turkey students walk to classes. There is still a shortage of schools in rural areas.

Revolution Contending with a Huge, Bleak Land

The revolution in jobs, customs and religion that Atatürk hoped would sweep Turkey is just beginning to make its way across Anatolia, the country's vast Asian homeland. Most of Anatolia is a harsh and difficult region where men struggle for simple survival. Roads are few; goods and people move by oxcart; and the peasants, who constitute the vast majority of Turkey's population, are perforce locked into the past. Illiteracy remains high and production low. But change is overtaking the land. Today it affects the larger towns and more prosperous farms. Tomorrow, Turkish leaders hope, it will reach the villages.

PRUNING VINES, trousered women work in a vineyard near Izmir. Grapes and raisins produced from such well-tended western vineyards are exported from Turkey in great quantity.

DRAWN BY OXEN, farm workers pass a field *(left)* in west-central Turkey. Although mechanization is reaching the farms, animals and humans are still the major rural power sources.

TRANSPLANTING TOBACCO, workers move seedlings from a field near Izmir. To protect the quality of Turkish tobacco, the Government restricts the area in which it can be grown.

LARGER TOWNS, gradually modernizing, are still struggling with the problem of poverty

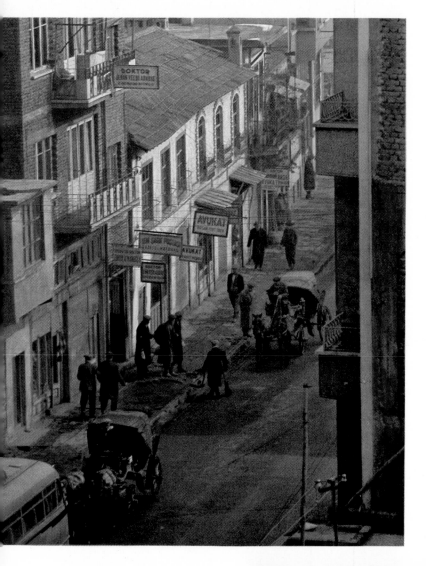

STREET SIGNS advertise the services of lawyers and doctors in Diyarbakır *(above)* in the southeast. Turkey has only one doctor per 2,750 people. Peasants usually travel to the towns for medical help.

SHOESHINERS work from elaborately fashioned boxes on a street corner in Diyarbakır. Since other work is unavailable many men eke out a living at such jobs. The region suffers from severe poverty.

96

GROUPS OF WORKERS wander along the main street *(above)* of Niğde, a farm town in the south. Electric-power lines *(background)*, water systems and paved roads are now coming to the larger towns.

HORSE-DRAWN TAXIS provide much of the transportation in Erzurum, but motorbuses *(background)* are beginning to replace them. Railroads and radio are slowly linking eastern towns to the outside world.

97

LIMESTONE CLIFFS of Pamukkale in the southwest drop 325 feet from the top of a plateau *(above)*. The cliffs—site of an ancient Roman bath—were formed by the action of hot springs.

EARTHEN HOUSES of the village of Harran *(left)* in the southeast resemble clustered anthills. The Bible records that Abraham spent some time in Harran on his journey to Canaan.

EERIE VALLEY of Göreme in central Turkey is jagged with cones, pyramids and needles that were formed by water erosion working on soft volcanic debris. The peculiarly shaped rocks were hollowed out in ancient times by hermits and members of religious sects. The earliest Christians in Anatolia built hiding places inside the rocks. Some of the rocks are still inhabited.

WOMANLY CRAFTS, which helped to keep the villages self-sufficient through many centuries, have not yet fallen into disuse

LOP-EARED CAP is admired by village boys in the east. Most of the clothing that villagers wear today is made from factory-produced fabrics. The women sew it to their own patterns.

WELL-SWADDLED BABY is rocked to sleep by his mother *(below)* in Eski Antalya on the southern coast. About three quarters of Turkey's population lives in such small villages.

HOUSEHOLD LOOM is expertly operated by an elderly woman. In some areas of Turkey carpet weaving is practiced in almost every home. Thread is spun from sheep's and goat's wool.

SHY KNITTER makes a white garment in the eastern village of Van *(opposite)*. Many village women knit socks and vests for the family and often work at spindles between other chores.

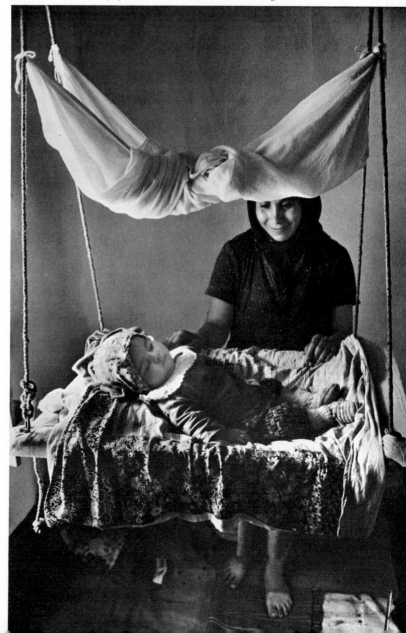

7

Struggle toward Democracy

POLITICAL democracy is a revolutionary idea in the Middle East, which was so long dominated by the Ottoman Empire. By the time that empire reached its zenith, in the 16th Century, the ideal of government by the people for the people had long been gone from the Greek-speaking world that had given birth to the democratic principle. The Christian emperor in Constantinople, in the words of one scholar, had been "the single figure in which were exhibited the two complementary offices of men, sacred and secular." The sultan-caliphs, like the emperors before them, were autocrats whose least word was to be obeyed. The concept that there could be a loyal opposition to a ruler regarded as "the shadow of God upon earth" was unknown in a society that justified the slaying of royal brothers in order to preserve undivided rule.

This is not to say that there were no checks on the Sultan's power. Theoretically, the only source of law was the revelation of God; the Sultan was as much under law as any of his subjects. The members of the Moslem judiciary, as interpreters of the *Seriat,* or revealed law, therefore had considerable influence on the Sultan's actions. So did some of the more outstanding viziers, or executive ministers, who served the Sultan. Yet the viziers had to be careful. About 10 per cent of them were executed after removal from office, and during the 16th Century reign of one Sultan, Selim the Grim, it became habitual for viziers summoned hastily to the royal presence to write their wills before keeping the appointment. A more effective barrier to despotic tendencies in the ruling house arose in the powers acquired in later centuries by two other groups: the Janissaries, whose armed strength gave their periodic revolts an imposing seriousness; and the "valley lords," whose sway over feudal estates in the Balkans and Anatolia made them a force to be reckoned with.

THIS background is to be held in mind in order to understand the break in tradition represented by Atatürk's espousal of the democratic theory. The first President of the Turkish republic had grown to manhood at the end of the 19th Century, a period during which the central power of the Sultans had been increased by the destruction of the Janissaries and by the elimination of traditional balances and checks; in the same period the renewed despotism of Sultan Abdül Hamid had administered a devastating blow to the democratic ideas that had gained a foothold in the empire.

During his lifetime Atatürk employed the forms of democracy, as we have seen. Yet his attempts to fill these forms with life collided both with autocratic elements within himself and with hard-to-remove obstacles in the social reality of his time.

As early as April 23, 1920, less than two weeks after the Sultan had dissolved the last Ottoman parliament, Atatürk convened a new parliament in Ankara, which had become the headquarters of the nationalist struggle. It was called the Grand National Assembly, and its purpose was "to secure the independence of the country and to deliver the seat of the Caliphate and the Sultanate from the hand of our enemies." On January 20, 1921, the same assembly passed the Law of Fundamental Organizations, declaring that "sovereignty belongs without reservation or condition to the nation; the system of administration rests on the principle that the people personally and effectively direct their own destinies." Thus sovereignty passed from the Sultan to the Turkish people.

This protoparliament was to be used by Atatürk as an instrument in his own grand design. But like any large body of men undisciplined by terror, the assembly naturally tended to split into factions.

While Atatürk hoped for a speedy declaration of a republic, some of his closest associates in the war of Turkish survival—conservative democrats like Prime Minister Rauf Orbay and the military commander Refet Bele—argued that the sultanate should be transformed into a constitutional monarchy rather than abolished.

By 1923 the Sultan had been deposed and the Greeks had been expelled from Turkish soil. With the shaping of Turkey's future now the problem at hand, the conservative composition of this first hastily summoned parliament seemed a menace to Atatürk's plans. New elections were ordered and a new assembly, more amenable to Atatürk's policies, was convened in Ankara in August of that year. Rauf Orbay, who had grown increasingly wary of Atatürk's dictatorial bent, resigned the post of Prime Minister. He was replaced by Fethi Okyar, another close colleague of Atatürk, and a man who he judged would prove more pliable than the strong-willed Rauf.

WITH his political backing consolidated, Atatürk pressed ahead with his goal of making Turkey a republic. After less than three months in office Fethi and his Cabinet followed Atatürk's orders and resigned, precipitating a Cabinet crisis. On October 29, 1923, Atatürk suggested to the parliament that the only solution to such crises was to strengthen the Cabinet by proclaiming a republic. After only hours of debate the assembly approved the resolution, and the Republic of Turkey at last came officially into being. Atatürk was immediately elected its first President. Ismet Inönü, negotiator of the Lausanne Treaty, which had recognized Turkey's victory in the war of survival, became the Prime Minister.

Backed by this new, apparently obedient assembly, Atatürk continued to have his way. On March 3, 1924, the caliphate was abolished and the last caliph was sent into exile. On April 20 a constitution was introduced that was to last until the military coup d'état of 1960. But later in the same year this assembly, too, began to behave in a democratic manner—that is, to divide into factions. Many of the men who had been Atatürk's devoted aides during the struggle for Turkey's survival as a nation began to argue that the dictatorial tendencies in their leader's nature should be resisted now that the emergency was over. Men like Rauf Orbay and the military leaders Refet Bele and Kâzım Karabekir argued that there would be no limit to Atatürk's authority until an opposition group was formed in the assembly. They organized the Progressive Republican Party, which began to harass Atatürk's own Republican People's Party.

ATATURK, whatever his theoretic belief in democracy, could not accept this atmosphere of argument. In June 1925, Kurdish mountaineers, resentful over the abolition of the caliphate and over the fact that the promise of an independent Kurdistan contained in the postwar Treaty of Sèvres (see Chapter 5) had not been honored, began a rebellion. It was quickly put down, but Atatürk used the outbreak as an excuse to suppress the opposition party.

So ended the first phase in Turkey's evolution toward democracy. The second phase was also to take place under Atatürk. It, too, was eventually to end in failure.

By 1930 there was a considerable ground swell of discontent in the country, not only because of Atatürk's secularist reforms, but because, in its effort to industrialize quickly, Atatürk's Government had neglected agriculture, the mainstay of the Turkish economy. In August 1930, therefore, Atatürk made an attempt to quiet the unrest by moving away from one-party rule. He ordered the formation of a new group, the Free Republican Party, and chose former Prime Minister Fethi Okyar as its head. He also encouraged his closest aide, Nuri Conker, and his own sister to join the new party. In a letter to Fethi Okyar the dictator claimed: "Since my youth I have been in favor of a system in which honest individuals and political parties would express and debate freely ideas in the Assembly or before the nation for the benefit of the country . . . consequently I consider it one of the bases of the Republic to have a new political party in the Assembly, which, based on similar principles, will debate freely the affairs of the nation." By the words "similar principles" Atatürk indicated the limits he intended to place on freedom of expression. The contending parties were to share an anticlerical, modernist viewpoint. Their debates, Atatürk clearly hoped, would keep pressure off him and leave him, as President, safe from the squalls

and constant concerns of day-to-day political affairs.

But the Free Republican Party succeeded too well. Everywhere its leaders went they were given tumultuous welcomes. Under pressure from his own Republican People's Party, Atatürk agreed to engineer the dissolution of its rival. Fethi Okyar himself, realizing that keeping the Free Republican Party in existence would lead him into collision with Atatürk, dissolved the party in November 1930.

Atatürk did not experiment again. For many years Turkey was to remain a one-party state. Only the forms of democracy were maintained. When Atatürk died in 1938, he was succeeded as President by his colleague in the war of survival, Ismet Inönü. In ensuing years prime ministers came and went. Inönü remained head of the Republican People's Party as well as of the state; the party became entrenched as the instrument of government; the powers of the police were increased; criticism was stifled.

The lack of democratic advance was justified, in the eyes of Turkey's leaders, by the international situation. They recalled the error of the Young Turks in entering World War I on the side of the Central Powers before the aims of the Young Turks' revolution could be consolidated. The outbreak of World War II, in 1939, came only a year after Atatürk's death. The major aim of the leaders of the Turkish republic—its institutions not two decades old, its economic transformation hardly even begun—was to avoid entanglement in the conflict.

ALTHOUGH they remembered Atatürk's advice to stick to Britain, because it would win, the Turks retained a certain admiration for the Germans. The struggle between Germany and the Soviet Union—heir to czarist Russia, Turkey's ancient enemy—increased public sympathy for the Third Reich's military campaigns in the east. While Nazi racial policies were not imitated in Turkey, there was discrimination against non-Moslem groups in the wartime years. These were years of economic strain for Turkey; the Government imposed onerous taxes that fell almost exclusively on the Greek, Armenian and Jewish citizens of the republic rather than on the Moslem majority. But Inönü wisely kept Turkey neutral until February 1945, when the country declared war on the Axis in time to qualify, at the last moment, for membership in the United Nations.

An organizer rather than a visionary, assiduous reader more than loquacious orator, Inönü deserves to be studied in his own right as one of the remarkable men of the century. The son of an Ottoman jurist, and a career soldier like Atatürk himself, Inönü was gentle, kindly, sober and unflamboyant. Also ruthless and stern when he had to be, he was able to efface himself in what he took to be his duty to the country he served as passionately as had Atatürk. In his adherence to the democratic ideals of the revolution and in his recognition after World War II that the time had finally come for Turkey to inaugurate true political democracy, Inönü was to go one step further than had Atatürk and allow elections in which his own party and his own rule were to be defeated.

THE foundation for this peaceful surrender of power was laid in 1945, when Inönü permitted parties other than his own ruling Republican People's Party to organize. The most important of the new organizations was the Democrat Party, founded by former Republican deputies. Two of these deputies—Celâl Bayar and Adnan Menderes— were destined to play an important and ultimately tragic role in Turkey's political development. Bayar had been Prime Minister of Turkey from 1937 to 1939, having taken the post after a quarrel between Inönü and Atatürk. Before that Bayar had played an important role in economic life as founder of the Business Bank. Adnan Menderes was an eloquent, dynamic politician from a wealthy, landowning family.

In its first try at the polls in 1946 the Democrat Party did badly, winning only 61 of the 465 seats in parliament. The Democrat defeat did not reflect public feeling; the Government used its prestige as well as its police to intimidate the voters. With great common sense the Democrat Party made the best of the situation and spent the next four years building up a formidable organization throughout Turkey, concentrating particularly on the neglected villages and small towns of Anatolia, where grievances and voters were most numerous. Still another factor in the forthcoming Democrat victory was Inönü's own integrity. Like Atatürk he had ruled highhandedly; in 1950 he insisted that the elections be conducted with strict fairness. In consequence of Inönü's impartiality the

Democrat Party was able to win a landslide victory, gaining 408 of the 488 assembly seats. Inönü's Government handed over power without demur.

This unprecedented obedience to democratic theory was probably Turkey's most glorious moment, the moment in which Atatürk's professed devotion to democratic processes seemed crowned with miracle.

President Bayar and Prime Minister Menderes were to manage Turkey's affairs for a decade. The way they did so was to bring ignominy to both. To Menderes came a tragic death; to the country as a whole came a sense of blighted hopes.

Propelled by a great wave of public support, the Democrat Party initially conducted affairs in a manner that enhanced Turkey's reputation abroad and accelerated growth at home. Turkey's prompt support of the United Nations' action in Korea, several record-breaking harvests, unprecedented investments in rural and industrial development, and a rise in per capita income induced a mood of euphoria, a sense that the country was playing a prestigious role abroad while prospering domestically. This mood changed to one of interrogation and doubt when years of drought coincided with accelerating foreign indebtedness as imports flooded the country without restriction. Studiously avoiding any sort of economic planning, the nation's rulers continued to borrow abroad and to spend freely on the construction of factories and other installations, which were often placed in locations calculated to win votes rather than in accordance with the realities of economics. By 1956 Turkey's foreign debt exceeded one billion dollars; inflation was rising.

MENDERES' situation was difficult. His victory at the polls had taken place not only because he had built a well-geared machine but because of the support of two separate categories of voters. One consisted of the moderate, educated citizens who felt that it was time for a change after more than a generation of one-party rule; the other was made up of the great mass of uneducated Anatolians who had basic grievances against Atatürk's reforms. These two groups had made very different criticisms of Inönü. The educated group objected to the restrictions on civil liberty imposed by a wartime though nonbelligerent Government. There was also considerable support among middle-class Turks for the promises made by Bayar and his followers that they would encourage the development of private enterprise and cut back on the Government's involvement in the economy.

But the popularity of Menderes among the second group, the villagers of Anatolia, rested on quite different factors. Not only did his changes mostly benefit the countryside rather than the cities, but he gave the simple peasants a considerable dose of what they most wanted—a return to Islam.

Since the 1920s Turks had been curbed in the practice of their faith. Fulfillment of the duty of pilgrimage to Mecca had been almost impossible. The call to prayer had been made five times daily in Turkish, not the "holy" Arabic of the Prophet. Theological colleges had been closed. The dervish orders suffered as wintry a time as had the religious orders in Communist countries. Now in June 1950—as a result of the first law passed by the Democrat assembly —the call to prayer was once more heard in the beautiful language of the Prophet. Turks began to go on pilgrimage again. Religious education in the public schools, restored on a voluntary basis by the Inönü Government in 1949, was made compulsory by the Menderes Government in certain primary grades. In villages such sentiments as these were heard: "Splendid men, these Democrats! This year they're restoring religious lessons. Next year they'll give us back all the rest, Arabic letters and the fez. We'll throw away this cursed infidel hat."

A certain fervor revived a nation whose whole history had been linked with religion and that had felt numbed when cut off from it. Pictures of Turkish soldiers in Korea showed them holding the Koran.

Fervor among the peasantry was not shared by the Westernized elite in the cities. What delighted the peasants alarmed the educated group. After the Menderes Government had been in office for only a few years the educated people who had supported him in 1950 began to turn against him. Although Menderes regained power in the elections of 1954 and 1957, his hold on the ultimately decisive groups in the country—Army officers, educated people, journalists, students—gradually lessened. They criticized him for spending so wastefully that the country was on the verge of bankruptcy; they charged him with subverting Atatürk's reforms by encouraging reactionary religious movements. The talkative coffee shops in the cities rumbled with indignation while in the countryside the Prime Minister's prestige, far from being lessened, acquired a near-religious glow.

THIS was the crucial moment. If Menderes had played the democratic game with rigid fairness, he might have lost one election and swung back to power in another. But Menderes could not resist the temptation of using his popularity with the uneducated Anatolians to maintain his hold on power by a mixture of fair means and foul.

Menderes and some of his political colleagues became pathologically sensitive to criticism. In 1953 the administration began to pass a series of increasingly restrictive laws designed to silence detractors. When the academic community became disenchanted with the Democrat administration, all professors were ordered to refrain from political activity. All judges who had served more than 25 years were

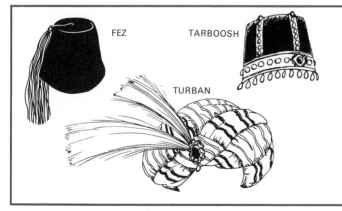

THE SYMBOLISM OF TURKISH HEADGEAR

Changes in Turkish headgear corresponded to major phases in the country's history. The earlier Ottoman Turks wrapped their heads in elaborately folded turbans to distinguish themselves from non-Moslems. After conquering Constantinople they adopted a decorated Byzantine skullcap called the tarboosh, but covered it with a turban to signify "right of conquest." In the early 1800s Sultan Mahmud II labeled the turban a symbol of reaction and banned it in favor of a cylindrical, tasseled hat called a fez. The fez, in turn, also came to symbolize reaction and was banned by Atatürk.

ordered to retire to open the way toward placing supporters of the regime on the bench. The Government gave itself the right to dismiss civil servants without appeal. Laws were passed permitting the closing of newspapers and the jailing of newsmen for the appearance of any item deemed harmful to the political and financial prestige of the state or even "damaging to public confidence in the government." Between 1954 and 1960 more than 200 newsmen were fined or imprisoned, and more than 1,000 were brought in for questioning by the police.

SIMILAR tactics were used against the opposition parties. Political meetings were prohibited except during a 45-day period prior to elections; any type of electioneering was also restricted to this period. Police were given the right to fire at crowds assembled in "unlawful political activities." In 1957 the Government began restricting the assembly itself. Deputies were limited in the number and scope of questions they could ask of Cabinet ministers, parliamentary immunity was restricted, and newspapers were forbidden to report on "subjects of an offensive nature," even if the subjects were up for assembly debate.

Attention was distracted from internal difficulties by an external problem that aroused Turkish national feelings. The island of Cyprus lay visible off the southern coast of Anatolia. It had once formed part of the Ottoman Empire; now a British crown colony, it contained a large, Turkish-speaking minority. In the mid-1950s the island's Greek-speaking majority, demanding *enosis*, or union with Greece, was fighting a guerrilla campaign against the British. Menderes took an active role in sponsoring the claims of the Turkish minority, who countered the Greek campaign by demanding partition of the island and union of the Turkish-speaking areas with Turkey. After years of fighting, Menderes traveled to London in 1959 to conclude an agreement among Britain, Greece, Turkey and the two Cyprus communities providing for the island's independence. His airplane crashed outside of London, but Menderes stepped from the ruins, to be offered a cup of tea by a solicitous British housewife. His miraculous escape (15 of the 25 other passengers died in the crash) placed the Prime Minister of Turkey in a context

familiar to traditional Eastern piety: he was the man on whom the beneficence of God had visibly set its mark. As Menderes drove into Istanbul after his return from the English capital, the road from the airport to the city was lined by peasants waiting to slit the throats of sacrificial sheep. Menderes had become something close to a messiah—to himself as well as to his supporters.

Menderes now fell victim to that spiritual blindness diagnosed by the classical Greeks as the prelude to nemesis. He began to identify his opponents with evil. In his infatuation Menderes was not helped by his entourage, men with none of his panache. They were instead often distinguished solely by an obsession with quick profits, an interest that filled the coffeehouses with gossip.

Economic chaos, curtailment of civil liberties and the stern line Menderes adopted with students who launched a series of protest riots in the spring of 1960 gave a group of Army officers reason enough to stage a coup d'état on May 27 of that year. Menderes, his Cabinet and all the Democrat deputies were imprisoned and arraigned for trial.

THE coup had been launched by a junta claiming to act in defense of the Kemalist revolution and under the apparent leadership of Cemal Gürsel, the former Commander of Land Forces of the Turkish Army. They claimed that they had instituted a revolution, not carried off a putsch, and that they intended simply to continue the democratic development that the abuses of Menderes had halted.

Menderes and his fellow prisoners were placed on trial on the island of Yassıada, which lies off Istanbul in the Sea of Marmara, within sight of the city's mosque-ridden skyline. The trials began in October 1960; they did not end until September of the following year. The 202 sessions lasted 1,033 hours. There were 592 defendants and 1,068 witnesses. The judicial procedure was comparatively fair, but all political trials leave an observer with the uneasy feeling that such performances have little basis in legality. The military men accusing Menderes and his partners of violating the Constitution had themselves acted unconstitutionally in their coup d'état: Atatürk's Constitution gave the members of the military no right to dispose of governments they disliked.

The charges at the trial ranged from the trivial to the serious. The accusation that most caught public attention involved a dog presented to President Bayar by the King of Afghanistan. Bayar was accused of having committed a corrupt act in selling the dog to a state zoo. He had indeed sold the dog to the zoo, but the money realized from the sale had been spent on a fountain for a village near Izmir, and the deposed President's nonchalant attitude to the charge —"It was not," he said, "an important matter"— won him widespread sympathy. Such "corruption" might have outraged a Scandinavian public; but Eastern electorates still expect a statesman to dispense gold like Zeus—to be, in a word, above the law.

MENDERES was accused of trying to engineer the death of his illegitimate child (he was acquitted on this charge), of using public funds for personal expenses, of ordering illegal measures used against Inönü and his party, and of a host of other crimes. Perhaps the charge with the gravest international implication was that Menderes, Bayar and others had organized riots against the Greek communities of Istanbul and Izmir in the autumn of 1955 for the purpose of exploiting public feeling over Cyprus to distract attention from Turkey's economic troubles. The riots had been touched off by reports that a bomb had damaged Atatürk's old home in Salonika. The charge that the former leaders had planned the bombing was not proved, but it became clear from the trial that they had in fact incited the riots.

Menderes' mythopoeic power over the Turkish masses was diminished neither by the crimes with which he was charged nor by his abject behavior at the trial. While he was held under maximum security guard on Yassıada, simple people in Turkey believed that he rode nightly on a white charger to pray at the Eyüp mosque above the Golden Horn.

The continued popularity of Menderes probably led to his execution. Despite the junta's endorsement of a new constitution designed to render impossible another Menderes-type dictatorship, almost 40 per cent of the voters rejected it in a referendum held in July 1961, an indication of the persistence of sympathy for the deposed Prime Minister. In September of that year 15 of the defendants, including Menderes and Bayar, were sentenced to death. Bayar was spared (on grounds of old age) and the sentences of 11 of the condemned defendants were commuted to life imprisonment. But the verdicts against the Prime Minister and two of his most unpopular ministers were carried out. Menderes' hanging was gruesome; the victim had been revived from an attempt at suicide not long before.

The killing of Menderes was doubtfully justified in law; in policy it was ill-omened. Although the junta kept its promise and there were free elections in October, there was no clear endorsement of the 1960 "revolution." None of the contending parties received a majority; the newly formed Justice Party, widely regarded as the successor to Menderes' proscribed Democrat Party, won some 35 per cent of the vote. Gürsel became President; Ismet Inönü, whose Republican People's Party garnered some 37 per cent of the ballots, became Prime Minister. A series of impotent coalition Governments followed. All that had emerged from the experience was the realization that the real power in Turkey lay with the Army. All politicians could now feel that over their heads was an extraconstitutional factor, the officers' corps, whose members might intervene on the national scene if a result at the polls or a policy put into practice should displease them.

ON a second, more dangerous level the threat to Turkish democracy was graver. The lesson that the Army possessed the ultimate authority in Turkey had a rider: whoever controlled the Army could make his own revolution. Cemal Gürsel was in the tradition of Atatürk and Inönü; having made his protest against Menderes he plainly wished to restore democratic practice.

But other members of the officers' corps had other ideas. In 1962 and 1963 ex-Colonel Talât Aydemir, resentful that the military junta had returned power to a Government of civilians, launched two unsuccessful coups; pardoned for the first, he was executed for the second. But the strains in the body politic might someday result in the seizure of power by some other extremist—of the Right *or* the Left—who could make his coup succeed. The only obstacle to such a tragedy remained an intangible factor—the good sense of the Turkish people.

HAILING VOTERS, Adnan Menderes is surrounded by a worshipful mob during an election campaign. His Democrat Party won votes by promising to relax the restrictions on Islam.

Division and Violence in National Politics

In 1945 President Ismet Inönü declared that Turkey should abandon the one-party system of politics that had served the country for two decades. In 1950 the Democrat Party led by Adnan Menderes came to power. Menderes proved a dangerous leader: he fomented riots for his own purposes, banned public meetings and incurred vast international debts. The military deposed him in 1960, and he was executed the following year. But clashes between his former supporters and the military have kept politics in turmoil, a turmoil that has been compounded in recent years by the explosive Cyprus quarrel.

RUMBLING INTO ISTANBUL, Government tanks make a last-ditch show of power to discourage protest riots in early 1960. The 10-year Menderes regime had repressed all opposition.

CLAMORING FOR REVOLT in May 1960, university students throng the streets of Istanbul *(left)* to protest the assumption of dictatorial powers of arrest by Menderes' regime.

AWAITING TRIAL, Menderes *(below, right)* faces an interrogator of the new military regime. He was charged with violations of the Constitution and was hanged in July 1961.

*THE MILITARY has become
a key political force
in the turbulent aftermath
of the Menderes regime*

A NEW CONSTITUTION is framed in Ankara
in 1960 by a committee of professors appointed
by the military regime. Promulgated in 1961,
the Constitution created a senate, established pro-
portional representation to encourage opposition
parties and clearly guaranteed individual rights.

CONFIDENT LEADERS of the provisional Government cluster around General Cemal Gürsel
(*below, center*), who became Prime Minister and
Minister of Defense. The provisional Government banned political activity until 1961, when
a new election brought Ismet Inönü to power.

INSURGENT TROOPS move with fixed bayonets through Ankara during an unsuccessful attempt at another Army coup in 1962. The military has been frequently condemned by the new Justice Party, which has inherited a great many of the supporters of the outlawed Democrat Party.

RIOT SQUAD of Army troops prevents a clash in 1963 between supporters of the Justice Party and students *(below)*. The disturbance followed Inönü's accession to the Justice Party's demand that imprisoned Democrats be released. The officers' corps has increasingly intervened in politics.

GREEK LEADER, Archbishop Makarios, President of Cyprus, addresses a crowd of student supporters in Nicosia, the island's capital. Cyprus was given independence by Britain in 1960. In 1963 a bitter conflict broke out between its 500,000 Greek-speaking citizens and 100,000 Turkish-speaking citizens. Turkey and Greece threatened to go to war over the island strife.

RETREATING TURKS abandon their village *(above)* in
ruary 1964 after a battle in which a dozen people were ki
The fighting was finally interrupted by troops from Br

...es on the island. Later in 1964 a peace-keeping force un-
... United Nations auspices achieved an uneasy truce—broken
... sporadic clashes—but gained no resolution of the crisis.

*A SAVAGE FEUD on the island
of Cyprus has repeatedly brought
Turkey to the brink of war*

TURKISH LEADER, Dr. Fazıl Küçük, the Cypriot Vice
President, talks with a group of Turkish Cypriots at a refugee
camp. After the fighting began, the agricultural economy of
the island suffered drastically, and food supplies became short.

BRITISH TROOPS move into a coastal village *(left)* to halt
an outbreak of fighting. Greece has urged a revision of the
Cyprus Constitution that would leave the way open to union
with Greece; Turkey has favored a partition of the island.

Opera lovers join the stars in song in the lounge of the Opera House in Ankara. Western music has a large following in cities and is o

...eard on radio broadcasts. Native music nevertheless remains popular.

Acceptance of the West

AS the possessor of an extraordinarily rich historical heritage, Turkey is unique among the nations of the world in the conscious way in which it has accepted the West almost in its entirety. The country's awareness of its acceptance of Western modes, manners and thinking, whether in the arts, literature or political alignment, is particularly remarkable. Unconscious Westernization, a result of the immense preponderance and vitality of 20th Century Western civilization, is found in nearly every developing country. Equally, a conscious acceptance of certain Western technical innovations offset by a deliberate retention of certain spiritual or cultural values characterizes societies as varied as those of India, Japan and Egypt. In Turkey the over-all acceptance of the West seems unqualified by a struggle to retain traditional customs, costumes or attitudes. Naturally, traditional attitudes continue to persist; equally naturally, in a society based on the Western concept of nationalism, events of the past that reflect glory on the Turkish nation are remembered with pride. The year 1953 marked the 500th anniversary of the capture of Constantinople, the Byzantine capital, by Mehmet II, one of the great Ottoman Sultans. The event was widely commemorated in Turkey; colorful postage stamps were issued; pageants were staged by students dressed in the scarlet robes and high hats of Janissaries, the elite troops of the Ottomans. On such occasions as the annual celebration of the establishment of the Turkish republic, boys perform dances in public squares wearing fancy-dress turbans.

In everyday life, by contrast, Atatürk's clothing reforms have taken complete hold of the entire educated class—to start with the most obvious, if least essential, aspect of Westernization. Only in rural areas of Anatolia can traditional peasant dress be seen alongside Western clothing. A few miles in any direction outside Istanbul it is possible to see women dressed in vivid, multicolored, baggy pantaloons, and in many regions men favor colorful shirts and pants styled like riding breeches. But in the cities almost all Turks wear Western dress.

IN literature, difficulties have developed for the Turkish reader who wishes an acquaintanceship with his country's past. These difficulties are largely due to the removal of the Arabic alphabet, but also to the change in the language. It is as though a Frenchman found himself incapable of reading the works of Victor Hugo or as though an American were to find the Gettysburg Address extraordinarily difficult to understand. Everything printed before 1928 is as unintelligible to younger Turks as printed Chinese is to an Italian. Only when the works of an earlier Turkish writer are reprinted in the Latin alphabet can his words be understood; even then many works would require extensive footnotes to explain the Ottoman idioms and ideas—for classical Turkish literature is not alien simply because of its form. Much of its content has little meaning to the modern Turk. Elaborate poetry—whose virtue was the way it said things rather than the things it said— is of little interest. Even the Ottoman historians, who wrote in a chronicle style that is no longer fashionable in Turkey, have little interest for a generation whose schooling has made them demand at least a superficial Western smoothness in the manner of reporting on historical events.

Just as Atatürk wanted to drag Turkey into the family of Western nations, so some Turkish thinkers have tried to make Turkish culture part of the mainstream of the West. One influential writer has been Sabahattin Eyüboğlu. In an essay published in the newspaper *Cumhuriyet* a few years ago, Eyüboğlu attempted to prove that the Turks were part of the Western fabric by citing the myth that the Trojan hero Aeneas had, after the fall of Troy, migrated from Anatolia to Italy and become a remote founder of Rome. Citing the French essayist Michel de Montaigne as his source, Eyüboğlu quoted from a letter Mehmet II, the 15th Century conqueror of Constantinople, is supposed to have written to the Pope: "We too, like the Italians, are of Trojan stock. It is as much their duty, as it is mine, to take Hector's revenge from the Greeks." Eyüboğlu went on to claim that during the war of Turkish survival Atatürk himself, after a victory over the Greeks, had said: "At Dumlupınar we avenged the Trojans on the Greeks!" Both the accuracy of the quotation from Mehmet II and the authenticity of the statement attributed to Atatürk can be disputed. Eyüboğlu nevertheless employed both quotations to show that the Turks shared Homer's *Iliad*, that basic Western epic.

"Everything that comes to us from the west— plays, films, even advertisements for petrol—has been affected by the *Iliad*," Eyüboğlu claimed. "Every intellectual in the west knows it practically by heart. And yet this *Iliad*, whose heroes and even whose story we only know imperfectly, is an Anatolian epic. Homer, who is considered to be the father of the world's poets . . . is a son of Anatolia. Troy . . . is on the ground that was [wet again only recently] with the blood of the people of Anatolia fighting against their enemies. . . . And yet . . . our [clergymen] have even forbidden us the epics derived from our own country. For hundreds of years they've made us bow toward their Meccas and . . . their Baghdads."

EYUBOGLU hastened to state that Atatürk had focused attention on the Anatolian homeland. But there was, he implied, a danger of Turkey's being enslaved to the East on another pretext: some theorists want the Turks to look to a farther East, to that "Turan" beyond the river Oxus whence the Turks derived. Eyüboğlu strongly objected to that idea. The modern Turks, he argued, should embrace, through their Anatolian roots, that Western culture of which Anatolia was once an integral part.

Yet that much-vaunted Western civilization can scarcely appear an unclouded mirror to the Turks. To the people in the cities, and to those who can read, Western civilization must loom like so many mountaintops rising above a mist. It is true that a huge range of authors has been translated into Turkish. Many European writers were rendered into Turkish in the 19th Century; as recently as 1965 James Baldwin's *Giovanni's Room* was translated into modern Turkish. Homer himself has been translated into Turkish. But few contemporary Turks who read in translation the works of Homer, Charles Dickens or Jean-Paul Sartre have any very clear understanding of the roots in Christian theology and Greek philosophy from which these authors derive, or against which they react.

TODAY, young writers who have been influenced by Western authors—and every writer of prominence has been so influenced—are not entirely free agents in their writing. "The Republic," the Turkish scholar Kemal Karpat has observed, "prescribed certain conditions under which creative work would be protected: it must condemn the old regime, glorify nationalism and modernism, promote patriotism, inculcate the ideal of personal sacrifice for the common good."

Turkish writers have not always inculcated the lessons that society demanded. Some have been heterodox.

The works of the best modern Turkish poet, Nazım Hikmet Ran, were long taboo in his own country. Having spent much of his life in Turkish jails for his Leftist opinions, he fled in 1951 to Russia, where he died in 1963. Despite Hikmet's political history, he, as much as other, less controversial poets, shows the influence of poets of other traditions, whether the Spaniard Federico García Lorca, the Frenchman Louis Aragon, the Russian Vladimir Mayakovsky or the American-Englishman T. S. Eliot. Hikmet's *Plea* allies striking imagery with simple didactic affirmation:

This country shaped like the head of a mare
Coming full gallop from far off Asia
To stretch into the Mediterranean
　　　　　This country is ours.
Bloody wrists, clenched teeth, bare feet,
Land like a precious silk carpet
This hell, this paradise, is ours.

The form of cultural expression that has excited most interest among modern Turks is the theater. Here once more the total embrace of Western forms is what strikes the outsider. Unlike Japan—whose traditional Kabuki theater flourishes alongside an ultramodern industrial system—Turkey has made little effort to develop its traditional spectacles. It is not that Turkey lacked such spectacles. The *Orta Oyunu* was a centuries-old mime play with music, frequently described by visitors to Ottoman Turkey. Even more popular was *Karagöz*, a form of shadow play in which two-dimensional, gaily colored puppets performed a Turkish equivalent of Punch and Judy behind thin, transparent cloth. The Turkish scholar Sabri Esat Siyavuşgil in his account of *Karagöz* notes that the shadow dramas not only were witty and amusing but also were profound expressions of a Sufi, or mystical, way of thought. The 16th Century Turkish poet Baki used *Karagöz* to illustrate his philosophic ideas:

All life is controlled by the Master who
　　　　　remains behind the screen;
You surely do not imagine that these little
　　　　　figures move from free will?

Regrettably, *Karagöz* plays are no longer widely performed, as Professor Siyavuşgil himself has noted. What does exist—and with considerable vitality—is a theater that covers the usual Western range from opera (in which Italian operas are sung in Turkish) to musical comedy. *Death of a Salesman* is followed by *A Funny Thing Happened on the Way to the Forum*. The father of the modern Turkish theater is Muhsin Ertuğrul, who became director of the Istanbul Conservatory in 1927. He produced works by Shakespeare, Ibsen, Molière and Goethe, and also encouraged young Turkish playwrights to create works of their own. Today dramatists like Refik Erduran write essentially in the Western tradition. The quantitative expansion of the Turkish theater has been remarkable as well. Sixty-five new shows opened in Istanbul in 1964. While the Municipal Theater was performing *Turandot* in Turkish, Haldun Dormen, a graduate of the Yale Drama School, was rehearsing his closely knit troupe in a comedy of working-class life entitled *A Lover's Coming from Germany*. The play portrayed a prejudiced Istanbul family whose son expects the arrival of a "friend" recommended by a Turk working in Germany. He imagines a girl in a bikini. A bearded young man on a bicycle turns up instead. The family's concern over sex is gently satirized. An old woman has been kept sequestered all her life; when the German chases a butterfly she fears that he wants to rape her.

More important than the acceptance of Western dress and Western influences on the arts has been Turkey's acceptance of a Western political alignment. This was not an immediate result of the Atatürk revolution. In the years following World War I, when Turkey was struggling for its survival as a nation, its chief enemies were in Western Europe, and its main source of arms was Leninist Russia. But because of Communist ambitions inside Turkey,

KARAGOZ

HACIVAD

A TURKISH EQUIVALENT OF PUNCH AND JUDY

Centuries ago a form of popular puppet shadow theater known as *Karagöz* came to the Ottoman Empire from the Far East. Originally of religious significance, *Karagöz* later dealt with humor of everyday life. From behind a lighted screen the foot-high puppet Karagöz, a rough man of the people, would continually best his pretentious friend Hacivad in ribald situations. The *Karagöz* theater attracted large audiences, but recently, like other Ottoman vestiges, it has all but disappeared.

friendship with the Soviet Union withered before the death of Atatürk in 1938. During World War II —a struggle in which Turkey did not feel strongly committed to either side—the country remained neutral until February 23, 1945, when it made a technical declaration of war against the Axis, qualifying it for admission as a charter member of the United Nations. The postwar period was to make Turkey not merely an active member of the U.N. but a consistent advocate of Western policies.

In a sense the emergence of an intransigent and ambitious postwar Soviet Union restored the status quo between Russia and Turkey. Since the latter part of the 18th Century, Russia had been the chief enemy of the Turks. Twentieth Century Russia was to take up the expansionist aims that had moved the czars. Those aims had always included the acquisition of territory in eastern Turkey and the control of the straits between Europe and Asia. From the Turkish side, Communism was to be increasingly hated not only for itself but for its identification with Russia. The eastern Anatolian provinces of Kars and Ardahan had been seized by czarist Russia in 1878 and returned to Turkey by the Soviet Government in 1921. In 1945, when Stalin's Russia demanded the return of Kars and Ardahan, as well as a voice in the control of the Dardanelles, Turkey felt deeply threatened. Backed by the U.S. and the rest of the West, the Turks boldly rejected the Soviet demands. In the spring of 1947 the United States granted Turkey $100 million in military aid; in the following year the country was allotted $50 million in Marshall Plan funds and an additional $75 million in military aid. The association with the West against the Soviet threat was immensely popular in Turkey. Never neutral-minded, the Turks were delighted to be aligned against their traditional foe. Supported by its people, the Turkish Government made light of the consequent alienation of the Communist bloc and of some neutralist nations.

Turkey was to lose friends in another large area because of its *de facto* recognition of the new country of Israel in March 1949. This gesture, hailed as a promising example of realism in some Western circles, alienated Turkey's Arab neighbors, who regarded Israel as a creature of the West, one more imperialist intrusion into their territory.

If Turkish foreign policy alienated Communists, neutralists and Arabs, Turkish participation in the Korean War gave the country great stature in the United States and Europe. This was not due merely to approval of Turkey's support for the principle of collective action. The quality of Turkey's participation in the fighting was inspiriting. Not only did the Turkish soldiers win high accolades from American observers, but on occasions when they were defeated and captured they showed higher morale than did their American or British comrades.

TURKISH identification with the Western alliance culminated in 1952 when the North Atlantic Treaty Organization was expanded to include Turkey. At this time Turkey's reputation in the West probably stood higher than at any time since the age of Süleyman the Magnificent. Moreover, Turkey was willing to identify itself even further with Western goals. The United States had long wished to establish a regional defense system in the Middle East as an additional counter to Soviet aggression. The idea held great attraction for Turkey—and the country was quick to act on it.

The Baghdad Pact linking Turkey and Britain to Iraq, Iran and Pakistan was the fruit of a 1955 tour that Prime Minister Adnan Menderes made of several Arab countries. In promoting this ill-omened alliance Menderes was handicapped by three factors that wise counsel might have persuaded him to consider more closely before he started on his travels. First, Turkey was remembered in Egypt and other Middle Eastern countries as the imperial power that had controlled their destinies during centuries of neglect and backwardness. The last phase of Turkish rule in the Middle East had been scarred by severities that were still remembered. Second, Turkey had, as stated above, recognized Israel, the opponent whom the Arabs feared and hated more than the distant Soviet Union. Third, it was widely believed in the Arab world that Menderes' tour had been sponsored by the Western powers (it was certainly true that the idea of the pact had been initiated in the U.S. State Department, then under the direction of Secretary of State John Foster Dulles). The Western powers were widely distrusted in the region, not only for their support of Israel but, in the case of Britain and France, for imperialist records in the Middle East.

The idea behind Menderes' tour—the linking of an anti-Communist Middle East with Turkey and the Western powers—might have stood a slim chance of Arab support if the pact had been signed in Cairo, not Baghdad. But when Egypt, the pacesetter of Arab nationalism, rejected this military alignment, Menderes recruited Iraq, then under the direction of Prime Minister Nuri Said, as the sole Arab sponsor of his plan. In the other Arab countries Nuri Said, for all his ability, had long been regarded as a British puppet. His sponsorship of the alliance immediately made it the target of nationalist hatred in all other Arab capitals. In Baghdad itself the pact was unpopular from the start. The only direct result of Iraq's adherence to the alliance was to increase the Iraqi public's dislike of its monarchy and of Nuri Said. The violent deaths of Nuri, the King of Iraq and his uncle in 1958 were in part the result of Iraq's espousal of the pact in 1955.

Although the Baghdad Pact could scarcely have been considered a successful venture, it was nominally maintained after Iraq's secession from it in 1959 and even after the 1960 revolution in Turkey which ousted Menderes. The pact's emphasis was, however, moved from mutual defense to economic cooperation and the improvement of communications between members.

IN another area Turkey was confronted with a problem that was to prove more lastingly explosive than the situation in the Middle East. This was the island of Cyprus, which lies roughly 40 miles off Turkey's southern coast.

Cyprus had been an Ottoman province from 1571 (when the Greek-speaking Christians had welcomed Ottoman rule as a lesser evil than control by the ruling Venetian feudalists) to 1878. In that year the Sublime Porte surrendered the administration of the island to Britain in return for British support in a war with Russia, despite the fact that by that time 30 per cent of the Cypriot population consisted of Turkish-speaking Ottoman subjects. In World War I Britain annexed the island. Over the years many Turks left Cyprus for Anatolia, while many Greeks emigrated to Greece. By the mid-20th Century only about 18 per cent of the population was Turkish.

In the 1930s the Greek majority on the island began agitating for *enosis,* or union with Greece; and in 1954, soon after Archbishop Makarios became head of the community, the Greeks launched a guerrilla war against the British to achieve the union. In response, both mainland and Cypriot Turks insisted that if there was to be any change in the island's status, it should revert to Turkish rule. This demand was unrealistic, and the Turks soon began to agitate for a partition of the island. Questions of pride as well as of security were involved. The Turks saw it as an indignity for their Moslem brothers to be dominated by Greeks on a once-Turkish island. Turkish military men pointed out that the large Turkish Army was already strained, guarding frontiers with Bulgaria, Russia and the Arab countries. A Cyprus in potentially hostile hands would add a new area of danger, the exposed south coast, and it was true that there had been considerable inroads by Communist organizers among Greek Cypriot labor groups. There was in addition a strong Communist element in Greece itself.

Turkey's Western friends were in a quandary. The British administrators of the island—who long insisted that they would never give up the island—found that the Turks were the Cypriot community on which they could rely. A disproportionate percentage of the island's police was Turkish. The Turkish support for the British occupation—as an alternative vastly to be preferred to Greek rule—made the Greek Cypriots increasingly hostile to the Turkish. At the same time it was obvious to all that the Greeks wanted *enosis.* The second solution, that of partition, seemed impractical also, since the Turkish communities were scattered all over the island.

THE agreements under which Cyprus was given independence were concluded in Zurich and London in 1959. They went to considerable lengths to protect the status of the Turkish community on the island. Cyprus was to be an independent republic; but at the same time the Turkish minority was to have built-in privileges, including a 30 per cent membership in the legislature and in the civil service, as well as a Turkish vice president.

Soon after the agreements went into effect the Greek element on Cyprus began to show that it had accepted them only as a tactical measure. When it became plain that the Greek majority intended to treat the Turkish minority simply as a minority, whose status could be changed by the majority, the Turks on the island, supported by Ankara, refused to acquiesce in the Greeks' efforts to abrogate the Constitution. Fighting between the two communities broke out in December 1963, and the United Nations dispatched a peace-keeping force to the island. In August 1964, when the Greek Cypriots tried to take by force the only coastal area still firmly held by the Turks, the Turkish Air Force bombed Greek strongholds in the region.

As with so many similar problems, both sides were impassioned by the sense that they were wholly in the right. Again, as in many similar cases, conflict could hardly benefit either protagonist. Neighboring peoples, like the Russians and the Egyptians, who offered encouragement or arms to either side, had motives of their own that had little to do with the welfare of either Greek or Turkish Cypriots. The Egyptians sought Cypriot allies against Israel; Russia favored the disintegration of NATO, of which Greece, like Turkey, was a member.

FOR both parties to the island's squabble the Cyprus crisis was costly. Greece derived a considerable part of its income from tourism, and Turkey derived a little; tourism takes fright at the whiff of gunsmoke. Neither the Greek nor the Turkish economy could afford a military campaign. For Turkey's Western friends—friends and allies of Greece as well as of Turkey—the conflict over Cyprus was extremely damaging.

In the Arab world the policy of Menderes had needlessly aggravated relations. Over Cyprus the exploitation of legitimate Turkish pride on behalf of a community of some 100,000 Turks (about the size of a fair-sized Anatolian town) had strained not only the country's friendship with the United States but its alliance with Greece. Common sense demanded that the two neighbors should be friends; the tragedy of their quarrel lay in the fact that national pride and emotions had distracted both from a mutually shared goal: that of building a modern society.

A young girl does an impromptu twist for her parents and relatives in the modern home of the Aydınalp family in suburban Istanbul.

Increasing Prosperity for New Social Groups

Since 1923 Turkey has been engaged in the task of educating its people and modernizing the nation. The success of these efforts is difficult to measure. The illiteracy rate still hovers around 60 per cent. In trying to develop the economy, the state was hampered for many years by a paucity of foreign investments, an unwillingness to tax the peasant and the necessity of maintaining a huge military establishment. But in recent years, successful efforts to diversify the economy and a larger influx of foreign investments has gradually brought a measure of prosperity to businessmen and to laborers. State-run universities began to prepare more Turks for modern professions: medicine, engineering, law. Labor unions have been growing stronger; the position of workers has been improving. To an unfortunate extent, however, the traditional elite has monopolized the benefits of modernization. Spurred by its intellectuals, Turkey is now growing more aware of the necessity for a broader sharing of the national wealth.

YOUNG EMPLOYEES operate polishing wheels at a plant that manufactures glass near Istanbul (*above*). It employs 2,500 people—a number of them women. Jobs are plentiful for skilled laborers, but the unskilled labor market is glutted.

GLASS BLOWING in the plant is performed by skilled laborers (*below*). Turkey's industrial work force numbers 600,000. Roughly half are members of unions, although strikes were illegal until 1963. The average worker earns about $12 a week.

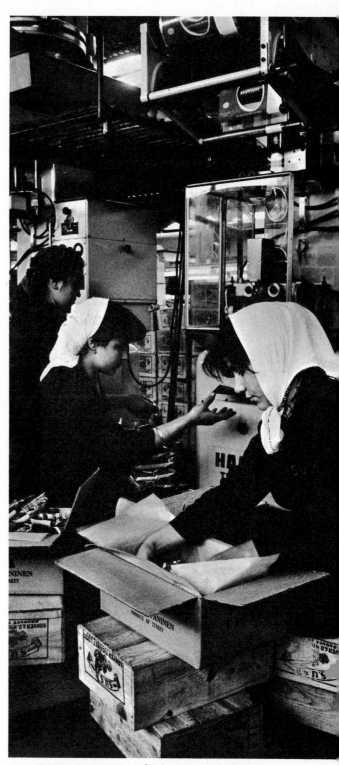

BOXES OF FRUIT are filled and sealed by a girl in a factory near Izmir. Rapid industrialization remains a primary goal of the state, but the development of agriculture and mineral resources is now receiving an increasing share of attention.

PLANT WORKERS, many of whom have made the leap from village poverty to the skilled labor market, constitute a new Turkish class

WOMAN LABORER loads a machine *(right)* in a cigarette factory in Adana. The tobacco industry is a Government monopoly. Under Atatürk the great majority of industries were state-run, but today private enterprise has taken the lead.

COASTAL STEAMER, which carries freight as well as passengers, is loaded *(below)* for a run from Istanbul to Iskenderun, on the southern coast. Turkey's ports are relatively unmechanized and provide a job market for unskilled laborers.

A MODERN FAMILY, the Pakyüreks follow a
Western mode of living that grows increasingly common

AFTER DINNER at home, Kemal Pakyür-ek, a prominent Adana cotton merchant, joins his wife and daughter in an English lesson. Many Turkish businessmen obtained their training in management techniques by working in state-run factories.

IN CONFERENCE, Pakyürek *(above)* discusses potential sales with his business partners. Personal prosperity has given businessmen like Pakyürek a voice in political affairs that was once limited to the administrative, religious and military elite.

IN THEIR APARTMENT, the Pakyürek and their son examine an album of photographs *(left)* taken during a trip through Europe. An increasing number of Turk of the upper and middle classes have been able to vacation abroad in recent years.

IN HIS FACTORY, Pakyürek watches the process of cotton ginning *(opposite)*, which the seed is separated from the fiber. More cotton is being grown in Turkey today because of a growing capacity to make yarn and cloth that can be sold abroad.

EDUCATION, public and private, is a crucial element in the nation's efforts at modernization

RESPONSIVE PUPILS attempt to attract their teacher's attention in a village class. Despite efforts to promote literacy, only two thirds of the country's children have access to schools.

UNDERGRADUATE LOUNGE at Ankara University draws students for discussions *(below)*. Turkey has four state-financed universities like Ankara with a total enrollment of almost 50,000.

ENGROSSED STUDENT, a young woman concentrates on an engineering problem at Robert College *(above)*. The university has graduated some of the nation's leading businessmen.

SHADED CAMPUS of Robert College *(opposite)* is situated in an Istanbul suburb. Supported by American donations, Robert College is the only important private university in Turkey.

DEAN OF THEATER, Muhsin Ertuğrul has been a leading actor and director for more than half a century. He pioneered in producing Western plays in Turkey.

LEADING EDITOR, Ahmet Emin Yalman for many years directed the Istanbul newspaper *Vatan*. He was several times jailed by criticism-sensitive Governments.

INFLUENTIAL WRITER, Mrs. Halide Edib *(left)*, who died in 1964, served with Atatürk during the war for independence. She wrote novels and war memoirs.

MODERN PAINTER, Bedri Rahmi Eyüboğlu works in a mosaiclike style. He founded the first modern movement among Turkish painters and has exhibited abroad.

POLITICAL COLUMNIST, Cetin Altan *(below)* is often openly critical of national policies. He was long a writer for *Milliyet*, a leading Istanbul daily newspaper.

NOVELIST OF VILLAGE LIFE, Yaşar Kemal works in his Istanbul apartment as his wife glances at a newspaper. Kemal is the author of the widely acclaimed *Memed, My Hawk*—a novel of brigandage and peasant poverty. It has been translated into eight languages. Kemal himself grew up in a village and for many years struggled at menial jobs before being published.

Dancing dervishes spin within a cloister in Konya in an effort to attain mystical union with God. The dervishes belong to one of the ma

Schism in the Soul

...eligious brotherhoods in Turkey that long enjoyed a great, popular following. They use music, as well as the dance, to achieve divine ecstasy.

FOR more than 40 years the tomb of Turkey's great mystic Celaleddin Rumi has been a garnished museum in the city of Konya. In display cabinets the visitor to Konya can see the flared white skirts in which the enraptured dervishes of times past whirled in their attempt, through the dance, to achieve unity with the divine. Disciples of the mystic sleep near him beneath embroidered coverings, each tomb surmounted by a high, woolen dervish cap. To complete the atmosphere a ghostly pipe pervades the museum with taped, liquid sound.

But except for foreigners, those who come to the shrine are not tourists. They are visitors paying homage to Mevlâna (Our Master, as the mystic is known to the faithful); they are not inspecting a museum. They throng to a Moslem equivalent of Lourdes, a place for prayer, intercession and, perhaps, miracle. As the Anatolian peasants shuffle in line past the labeled tombs, they pause, raise their hands, palms upward, and repeat the opening words of the

Koran: "Praise be to Allah, Lord of the Worlds, the Beneficent, the Merciful. . . . Thee we worship; thee we ask for help. . . ."

Mevlâna's shrine represents one pole in the Turkish spirit, for it is not only unsophisticated peasants to whom Mevlâna—in a sense the patron saint of Turkey—is an attraction. Suave young citizens from Ankara drive to Konya in Volkswagens or Chevrolets, disinfectants in their luggage, a little aghast at the backwardness of the plumbing in their own country's hinterland. But they, too, wish to visit Mevlâna's resting place.

THE other pole in the Turkish soul is the modernism that Atatürk admired, the goal that he set in his "Great Speech" of 1927, which took six days to deliver: ". . . make the people of the Turkish republic into a social unit which is completely contemporary and civilized in every way in every meaning of the word."

If it were possible to take the two nations in Turkey—the educated and the uneducated—and argue that Atatürk's ideas satisfy the first and the old religion satisfies the second, an analysis of the country would be simpler and its leaders' rule would be easier. If such a statement could be made, it might then be plausibly argued that as the 60 per cent of the population who are still illiterate become educated, Turkey's metaphysical problems gradually will be resolved.

Such a simplification is not valid; the problem and its answers are both more complex. The two poles exert pressure on the entire country. The peasants who apparently reject Atatürk's secularism and who provided the main support for Adnan Menderes' efforts to ease the restriction on the practice of Islam also revere Atatürk the leader; his portrait may be the one adornment of their coffee shops. The young intellectuals who seem in the mainstream of Atatürk's program—economists working on Turkey's Five-Year Plan or actors performing Ionesco's *Rhinoceros*—are often Moslems in more than name; many of them fast in Ramadan, the holy month of Islam.

Kemalism—as Atatürk's philosophy is known in Turkey—itself contains many ambiguities. Perhaps the Kemalist who most successfully resolved its ambiguities was Kemal Atatürk himself. His own metaphysics were simple: "Whatever conforms to intelligence, logic and the general good conforms to our religion." To the dervishes and preachers he was violently opposed—although more because of the reactionary political role they had played in the past than because of any metaphysical grudge: "Even if there were no laws to ensure this, no Assembly to ensure this, even if everyone withdrew from the struggle against those performing these perverse actions and I myself remained alone—I'd still go on cutting them down and killing them."

At least until the last years of his life Atatürk's most outstanding quality—his furnacelike energy—enabled him to combine trivial and grandiose elements in a complex integrity. In appearance he was a Western statesman. "Dressed as though for a conjuring act with white tie and gloves and top-hat," as an Australian woman journalist once pictured him, he relaxed for country life in the sports jacket and knickerbockers stylish for Western gentlemen in the 1920s and 1930s. But his private life was far from that of a country squire. At the dinners Atatürk gave for his cronies a blackboard would stand at one end of the room. A plentiful supply of raki (a Turkish spirit with an aniseed taste that has been compared to the milk of a tiger) was balanced by an even more plentiful supply of questions with which Atatürk, more schoolmaster than dictator, would bombard his guests. Food was often not served until midnight; guests were sometimes required to prepare essays to be read at the next dinner a week hence. Despite these long evenings Atatürk was famous for being at his desk early each morning. When not at his desk he would make long tours of the country—prying, probing, insisting that things get done. His rumored involvements with adolescents were only minor interludes in a lifetime obsessed with Turkey. The energy of the man, his will to power, held together diverse elements.

BUT even with Atatürk, there was no final harmony. "A rationalist without a rationalist philosophy," in the words of one of his biographers, the British author Lord Kinross, "he fell into moods of disillusion and despondency. A man of action with no actions left to perform, he fell back on the familiar substitute, alcohol; and this began to undermine his physical and mental condition."

Kemalism, to echo Lord Kinross' opinion of its founder, is a rationalism without a rationale. Even its oracles—the speeches and writings of Atatürk—have never been gathered into a "Complete Works." Very opposed interpretations of Atatürk's thought are possible, even on such apparently clear-cut economic questions as the choice between Socialism and free enterprise.

AT one end of the social spectrum Turkey's 19.9 million peasants are torn between a traditional faith and the cult of their dead leader, who is still revered for his role in saving a Moslem territory from Christian invasion. (Despite 40 years of lay government the colloquial word for foreigner remains "gavur," or infidel.) To the peasants each pole is blurred: religion is very near to superstition and Kemalism is hardly understood.

The strains at the other end of the spectrum—the educated elite in the cities—are even more severe.

In Turkey, as elsewhere, a purely rational interpretation of life—even when such is coherently advanced—satisfies few spirits. The hunger for God may be pushed aside when more immediate needs, such as the necessity for defending the group against attack or the search for food, impinge on men. But in a society that is even moderately prosperous or stable, men and women normally seek a purpose in life other than the satisfaction of national or bodily needs, just as those nearing death seek for some clue to the meaning of things and some explanation of the life they are about to leave. The Turks, with their long history of religious dedication, are no exception. What makes Turkey exceptional is that when the young or elderly Turk looks for spiritual guidance today he is at a loss.

At one extreme, religious development has been swaddled. For example, contact with that fountainhead of Moslem orthodoxy, the mosque-university of Al-Azhar in Cairo, has been almost nonexistent, so that pious Turks in general have little idea of how the university has been transformed. Turks are generally surprised when informed that women now study alongside men at Al-Azhar, and that science and engineering studies jostle with Koranic exegesis in the university curriculum. To all too many Turks, religious and irreligious alike, Islam seems opposed to the main currents of modern life.

Atatürk may have imagined that by suppressing or curbing Islam's devotional manifestations he would induce a relaxation of its grip on political and social areas of Turkish life. Another great rationalist, the historian Edward Gibbon, who wrote *The Decline and Fall of the Roman Empire,* argued that the "memory of theological opinions cannot long be preserved without the artificial help of priests, of temples, and of books."

Atatürk never tried to enlist the *hocas,* or village clergymen, in support of the revolution, although these simple people had been among his most fervent supporters during the war against Greek invasion. As a result, instead of becoming convinced that the modern world could be accepted and molded by Moslems, the *hocas* as a class were forced into a position of opposition to change. Their secret dream, shared with the masses whom they continued to guide, was a return to the "sacred" Arabic alphabet in which the Koran was written, the construction of mosques and the readoption of old-fashioned customs.

IF Atatürk, Gibbon and still another rationalist, N. Lenin, in fact had been correct, and religion had been a dying force, the naysaying of the *hocas* and the peasants would have mattered little to contemporary Turkey. But Turkey's majority religion, Islam, did not diminish in strength; it merely declined in intellectual quality. Religious solidarity accounted for much of the exemplary group morale that the Turks showed in Korea; religious faith remains the chief consolation of ordinary Turks in time of trouble.

Anticlericalism merely inhibited the emergence of a religious form capable of satisfying man's metaphysical needs; contemporary Turkey has so far produced no rethinking of religious fundamentals of the kind that has characterized Christian countries since the beginning of the Protestant Reformation. In consequence the confusion in the Turkish psyche persists.

At the other pole the development of a reasonable, rational philosophy has been equally difficult—

in part because of a continuing pressure exerted against those who do not find themselves in whole-hearted agreement with the official interpretation of the aims and meaning of Kemalism. There has been a consistent persecution, for example, of Turkish Leftists. This pressure against heterodoxy—which at times has paralleled the intolerance associated with the late Senator Joseph R. McCarthy in the United States during the late 1950s—has had unintended effects: on the accepted conventional level, there is an avoidance of thought, a conformism that aims only at preserving the conformists' material advance. Below this level, in an intellectual underworld, strange weeds have flourished.

AMONG those weeds is Pan-Turanism. Turanism derives from the name given to the ancient homeland of the Turks; its dynamic comes from the wish to unite all Turks, including those of the Soviet Union, in one state. The doctrine of Pan-Turanism won considerable allegiance in the early 1900s, when solution after solution was being proposed for the salvation of Turkey; it was repudiated by Atatürk, who confined his interests to the Turks living in Turkey. Nevertheless the idea has run like a subterranean current of irrationality below the aboveground structure of the republic. During the strained years of World War II some Right-Wing youth organizations were attracted by the ideas of racial purity and military glory espoused by the Third Reich of Nazi Germany. In 1942 a magazine called *Bozkurt (Gray Wolf)* nakedly presented this ideal: "It is the sacred aim of the Bozkurt Turkists to see the Turkish State become a nation of sixty-five millions. What will be your justification for that? We have long ago loudly proclaimed the principle involved in this matter: Right is not given, it is seized! War? Yes! War, when necessary! War is the great and blessed law of nature. We believe that war, militarism and heroism should be raised to the highest degree of reverence. . . ."

Generally regarded by moderate Turks as a lunatic fringe, the surviving Turanists represent only one brand of extremism. A Turkish Communist party was active in the early 1920s, when Turkish survival depended in large part on arms provided by Soviet Russia. The greatest obstacle to Communism at that time was public opinion, which regarded the

Communists as enemies of Islam and agents of Russia, the traditional enemy. As his control of Turkey became complete, Atatürk dropped his earlier tactics —of organizing a pseudo-Communist party loyal to himself—and overtly suppressed all manifestations of Communist thought. This policy was carried on even more rigidly by his successors. After the liberalization of 1946, when Premier Ismet İnönü allowed the formation of parties prior to the general election of that year, several Leftist groups emerged. Most important among them were the Socialist Workers and Peasants Party and the Turkish Socialist Workers Party. None of the Leftist groups were allowed to remain in existence more than a few months. Some clandestine Communist propaganda directed against the American-Turkish aid pact of 1947 nevertheless circulated during the period.

Turks were in no mood to respond to Communist propaganda. The Russian threat to Turkey was major; Turks showed their understanding of that threat only a few years later when the nation entered wholeheartedly into the struggle against Communist aggression in Korea.

In fact, nationalism and religion continue to be powerful forces; only in a Turkey where both had lost their appeal would Communism or extreme Leftism have presented a real threat. Both Islam and Kemalism—the forms that religion and nationalism take in the Turkish context—still possess great vitality. Moreover, there are signs that both forces can be restated in forms convincing to contemporary Turks.

ATATÜRK'S hostile attitude to religious institutions was in effect repudiated by the Democrat Party. When Adnan Menderes was overthrown on May 27, 1960, there was no clear return to Atatürk's position. The new President, Cemal Gürsel, stated in 1963 that "a nation without a religion is a group of animals." The change in emphasis from Atatürk's anticlericalism was significant.

An effort to restate the meaning of Kemalism was made in the fall of 1962 and the spring of 1963 at Istanbul's American-supported university, Robert College. There, members of Turkey's intellectual and political society gave a series of "Atatürk Lectures" under the auspices of the Faculty of Engineering.

Perhaps the most impressive speaker was Vedat Nedim Tör. By then in his sixties and an adviser to a Turkish banking firm, Tör had been a Communist in his student days. He believed, he said, that the Atatürk revolution had gone cold, and he evoked its great moments for his young audiences: "I wish you had lived in those days. The whole country embarked on a feverish campaign for literacy. Centers of instruction for the people were opened up in every town and village. Atatürk himself, in a state of dynamic ecstasy, traveled over the whole country, everywhere explaining to the people with a blackboard the difference between the Arabic alphabet and the Latin. Within six months, all books and newspapers appeared in the new alphabet and the Arabic alphabet was officially forbidden."

TOR indicated that he believed that a broad, popular education system could reconcile the traditional-minded to the aims of the revolution. "One of the great cultural achievements initiated by Atatürk," Tör said, "was the establishment of the People's Houses. These were progressive centers of popular education in a modern sense, offering young and old a wide range of activities and facilities: libraries, plays, art, folklore, sport and music. They helped young people in particular to spend their spare time profitably, instead of frittering it away in coffeehouses, on cards or drink. They helped to direct the people's enthusiasm toward various national problems and realities, to help them ponder the ideals of the revolution and thus to train a new, young Kemalist team. A few years ago an American expert was invited to this country to make a report on the steps necessary to promote popular education here. When he heard that the People's Houses had been closed, he said: 'I was going to suggest that you set up such institutions. Since you yourselves have torn down your own institutions, there is nothing more I can say to you.' The closing of the People's Houses and the Village Institutes is an example of anti-Kemalist barbarism and will be remembered with loathing in the history of Turkish culture and education."

These Robert College "Atatürk Lectures" were organized by students at a U.S.-style institution of higher learning that had developed far beyond the sectarian missionary college founded by the Congregationalist missionary Cyrus Hamlin a century before. In Sultan Abdül Hamid's time at the turn of the century, the student body had been almost entirely non-Moslem. During the early years of Atatürk's republic the college had continued to cater to non-Moslems and to the well-to-do. In 1960 it began offering an increasing number of scholarships to young men from all over Anatolia. In initiating a debate on Kemalism, Robert College was attempting to find a way toward the healing of the schism in the Turkish soul. The value of such an effort was only highlighted by its immediate failure. The lectures antagonized hooligan elements which at that time were breaking up any meetings that they could accuse of "Communism." The fact that Tör at one time had been a Communist was enough excuse for attacks on the lectures.

Despite the opposition to the conferences, the debate on the country's goals continues in Turkey today, for the country's need for a synthesis between the best in its own religious tradition and the best in Western technology and method is pressing. If such a synthesis is not achieved, Turkey may be torn between a reactionary form of Islam and a form of secular extremism. The result may be the emergence of some sort of extremist political regime.

A FORMAL nationalism is an increasingly barren substitute for a living faith; nationalism has also had the effect of isolating Turkey from its immediate neighbors. Any synthesis that does emerge may well restore Turkey's ties with peoples it once ruled, for a rediscovery of its religious roots will lead the country straight to the Arab world on its southern border. In addition, any new emphasis on the problems that Turkey shares with other developing countries is also likely to revive Turkey's connection with its neighbors. Such a correction of the balance within the country will not undermine what is valid in Turkey's modernization. In fact, in a better balance this modernization would prove the more significant. For the Middle East to which Turkey may return has in 40 years greatly changed. That region is itself working toward its own synthesis. It has already taken lessons in change from Turkey; in return it may give Turkey valuable lessons in continuity.

BOWING THEIR HEADS, the faithful pray in Edirne *(above)*. The five daily prayers of Islam have a specific sequence: the first at sunset, then at night, dawn, noon and afternoon.

Continuing Dedication to the Path of Islam

Today more than 98 per cent of Turkey's people follow the path of Islam. In village, town and city all activity comes to a standstill five times a day as the devout stop on the street, face the holy city of Mecca, where Mohammed was born, and prostrate themselves as they say their prayers in Arabic, the holy language of the Koran. Atatürk sought to break the hold of Islam, abolished the caliphate and outlawed the popular Moslem brotherhoods. Since 1950 many of his secularizing reforms have been repealed; Turks are again making pilgrimages to Mecca. But despite the revival of religion, church and state are at last separate—as Atatürk wished.

PERFORMING ABLUTIONS, Moslem worshipers wash their hands at a row of fountains outside the Süleymaniye Mosque in Istanbul. Washing before prayers is required by the Koran.

GATHERING AT NOON, worshipers recite prayers in the Blue Mosque in Istanbul *(opposite)*. Only a few Turks speak Arabic; most understand only the general intent of their prayers.

ORNATE MAUSOLEUM of Cela-leddin Rumi *(above)* in Konya in central Turkey is a shrine of the order of Dancing Dervishes. Rumi, a poet, storyteller and mystic, established the order in the 13th Century.

SPARTAN CHAMBER in Bursa, the burial place of many Moslem leaders *(left)*, is visited by devout women. A quiet city with many mosques and tombs, Bursa once was the Ottoman Empire's capital.

TOURING YOUNGSTERS troop down the steps of the Green Mausoleum *(opposite)* in Bursa, in which the remains of Sultan Mehmet I are buried. Turks regularly visit such reminders of past greatness.

ARABIC INSCRIPTIONS adorn the wall of a mosque in Edirne *(above)*. The very form of such writing has deep religious import for Moslems. The word "Allah" appears at the left.

SEATED CONGREGATION faces Mecca during a service in a mosque near Istanbul *(right)*. Worshipers alternately stand, sit cross-legged and press their foreheads to the carpeted floor.

YOUNG MATRONS stroll with their children along the streets of Bursa, its stores bedecked with Turkish flags for a national holiday. Only a few decades ago women would never have appeared unveiled in public, especially in Western clothing.

10

Questions for the Future

TURKEY'S conscious self-transfer from the mainstream of one tradition into that of another has been one of the most remarkable events of the 20th or any other century. The acceptance by the heirs of the Ottomans of Western ideals and methods has also been an unprecedented compliment to the West, in a period when insults to the West have been more common than compliments. The changes —made by Atatürk and his followers in the belief that they would benefit Turkey—were enthusiastically embraced by the educated minority in the country and passively accepted by the rest. The mood of euphoria that overlaid the country after Atatürk's revolution now, however, shows signs of turning to

one of weariness and doubt. Western methods have not solved the basic economic problems of the country, and Turkish public opinion wonders whether the compliment to the West has been appreciated. For the first time since the establishment of the republic in 1923, there is widespread question about Turkey's direction.

The dramatic nature of Turkey's shift in the 1920s can hardly be exaggerated. History provides no parallel of so total a movement of an entire society from one tradition to another. It is as though the England of Henry VIII had not merely closed its monasteries and broken with Rome but also embraced the manners and adopted the dress of the

Ottoman Empire, then the strongest power in Europe, or as though the United States had suddenly remodeled its way of life on that of imperial Japan. Other societies have adopted aspects of the Western tradition: the Republic of India has retained the parliamentary system bequeathed it by Britain; Nasser's Egypt has adopted as its way of survival the industrial system first developed in Europe. But India has retained its distinctive styles of dress and its indigenous cultural traditions. In Egypt the creed of "Arab Socialism" draws heavily on Islam. Only in Turkey has cultural Westernization been linked to political and military alignment with the West.

THE compliment to the West is thus indisputably a great one. For many centuries the Ottoman Empire was the adversary of Europe. Yet the heirs of the Sultan-Caliph scrapped their traditional dress, their alphabet, their past literature and their customs and moved into a military alliance with the nations composing that Western Christendom which in the past had been the perennial foe. At the same time, the modern Turks remodeled their institutions, professing a dedication to democratic ideals.

To the Turks this acceptance of the West meant two things. In the first place they were joining, they felt, a club of civilized nations. They were admitting at least tacitly the superior qualities of the group they had so long fought. After so many defeats drawn out over so many centuries they recognized that Western ideals and methods were more likely to make Turkey a prosperous nation than were the ideals for which, and the methods under which, its soldiers had fought so doggedly. They believed, in the second place, that political and military alignment with the West was the best protection for the Turks of Anatolia against their chief antagonists, the Communists who had succeeded to the control of czarist Russia.

Like all believers in a new dawn, the enthusiasts who supported Atatürk in the 1920s believed that they were closer to a new Turkey than they were in actuality. The years of effort that were needed to transform Anatolia shrank, in the fervor of vision, until it appeared to them that a few speeches would be sufficient to undo the neglect of centuries. Much of the euphoria endured after Atatürk's own demise

and after the period of pause during World War II. The adoption of all aspects of Western culture, from the ballet to the translated detective story, brought delight to many newly aware Turks who had come to feel that their old culture had been remote from the people at its best and suffocatingly repetitive at its worst. The years of Stalinist pressure against Turkey immediately after World War II demonstrated the value of the Western alliance.

The greatest single cause of the present disillusionment has been the failure of Turkey's rulers to solve the country's economic problems. Under Atatürk and İnönü only the foundations of an industrial economy were laid. Under Menderes, economic development was sped up, but in a haphazard manner that brought inflation and the accumulation of a crushingly large foreign debt. While members of the middle class became more prosperous, the village masses made relatively little advance.

The revolution of 1960 was in part inspired by disgust at the heedless extravagance and lack of economic planning of the Menderes regime. Perhaps the greatest accomplishment of the military regime that took over after the overthrow of Menderes was the establishment of the State Planning Organization in October 1960. It fashioned a long-term plan for economic development that was adopted by the Government which came to power in 1961 under Ismet İnönü. The plan's aim was ambitious: to relieve Turkey of reliance upon sorely needed foreign aid within a decade by bringing the economy to the point where further growth would be self-sustaining. Government, private and foreign investments were to be channeled into development programs that, the plan envisaged, would increase the gross national income by 7 per cent each year and at the same time would make some inroads on the defects in the country's socioeconomic structure.

SUCH goals would not be easy to attain. As in other countries, private investors tend to put their money into areas likely to realize relatively high, quick profits, avoiding commitments likely to return little more than a patriotic glow. An example of the problem facing Turkish economic planners was put forward not long ago by Professor Besim Üstünel, the former head of the State Planning

Organization. "In 1962," Ustünel observed, "private capitalists invested 3.6 billion Turkish liras [$400 million] in development; of this, two billion went into housing—not the kind of cheap housing which we require to rehouse the squatters in the environs of Ankara, for example, but in luxury apartments which bring in huge rents."

THERE are other areas of the economy in need of attention. The state-owned industries, which were launched in the 1930s in an effort to hasten industrialization, are badly in need of reorganization. Consisting of 22 major and 90 or so smaller enterprises, and controlling more than 40 per cent of the country's industrial life, these industries have long been operating under massive deficits.

Turkey's most pressing current problem, however, is its vast reservoir of unemployed and underemployed workers. Some 1.5 million Turks are now unemployed, and in the rural areas another four million men are idle much of the year. This current headache, compounded by the fact that Turkey's population is increasing at a rate of 3 per cent each year, makes it imperative that the economy be expanded to provide a decent livelihood for a growing population. Some relief is available in the increasing migration of Turkish workers to Turkey's partners in the European Common Market, of which the country became an associate member in 1963.

Any lasting improvements in Turkey's economic future, however, will depend primarily on advances in the agricultural sector of the economy, which still employs more than three quarters of the population but provides only 40 per cent of Turkey's national income. In the face of the population increase, output per man and yield per acre have been virtually stagnant since the 1930s. What increase in production has been achieved has been largely through the placing of new land under cultivation. Now the limit of expansion has been reached. The task is to increase agricultural yields through education of the tradition-bound peasant in modern farming techniques, by expanding the irrigation system, and by instituting soil conservation practices and a system of quality control over agricultural produce destined for export. Until Turkey's gradually expanding industrial capacity comes into its own, agricultural

produce will still be responsible for some 80 per cent of Turkey's export earnings.

Against a background of a mushrooming population and an antiquated economy, Socialist sentiment —often suppressed in former decades through a reflexive identification of Socialism with Communism —has in the past few years been permitted public expression. The most powerful of the handful of Socialist parties that burst upon the scene after the Army coup of 1960 is the Turkish Labor Party, led by Mehmet Ali Aybar, former law professor at Istanbul University. Educated in France before World War II, Aybar returned to Turkey in 1943, "profoundly impressed by France's collapse and the rottenness of its bourgeoisie." He began to preach and write about Socialism, was arrested a dozen times and was once sentenced to five years of hard labor but was released upon appeal. His party now claims to have more than 10,000 members.

TURKEY'S current unrest, stemming from frustration over the realization that modernization of the country is an infinitely more painful and gradual task than the Kemalists envisaged, has recently found an outlet for partial catharsis in a growing national self-assertiveness on the world scene. Many articulate Turks have begun to urge that a more "independent" role in the nation's dealings with the Communist bloc would impel the U.S. to increase its volume of aid to Turkey and bring in economic assistance from the Communist bloc as well. American aid has been large (some four billion dollars since World War II), but it has been expended mostly on assistance to Turkey's armed forces. Many Turks complain that Turks have received less per head than other Middle Eastern nations that have been less committed to the West.

Such sentiments did not reach the level of conscious complaint while Turkey's main obsession was with the defense of its frontiers against the Soviet Union. They attained wide expression in 1964, however, a year in which the Soviet leaders appeared committed to a continuation of the "soft" line initiated by Nikita Khrushchev, and a year in which tensions with Greece increased over the Cyprus question.

During the 1964 American Presidential campaign the Republican candidate, Senator Barry Goldwater, asserted that President Lyndon Johnson had committed a striking error: he had alienated Turkey, once the soundest of American allies. This statement was made the subject of banner headlines in the Turkish press. A great number of Turks indeed felt resentment at U.S. policy. Cyprus, they argued, was an island on their doorstep that might conceivably fall under Communist control; instead of supporting the Turkish cause, America seemed to be as eager to soothe Greek susceptibilities as to uphold its largest Middle Eastern ally.

Turkey's rulers—above all its then Prime Minister, the veteran Ismet Inönü—were far too aware of the realities of the international situation in the Balkans and the Middle East to make such arguments. They recognized that for the U.S. (as in fact for its allies) the maintenance of the over-all Western alliance was far more important than the specific way in which the Cyprus problem was resolved. To the outside observer, or to the experienced and balanced statesmen within the area, the overriding need was plainly for the contesting countries to resolve their differences.

But ordinary Turks could not argue so coolly. They felt that the way the situation was developing represented an assault on Turkish self-respect. They could not watch unconcerned while the rights of the Turkish community on the island—rights embodied in the Cyprus Constitution and jointly guaranteed by Greece, Turkey and Britain—were being destroyed by the dominant Greek community.

JUST as the Greek Government (equally aware of the need for caution) was swept to the support of the Greek Cypriots by Athenian crowds, so the Government of Ismet Inönü was swayed by crowds in Istanbul and Ankara. As the Greek Cypriot forces increased pressure on the Turkish Cypriots, Turkey threatened to invade the island. In an effort to apply pressure on Greece, Turkey abruptly expelled Greek nationals resident in Turkey in the spring of 1965. Earlier, the Turkish Foreign Minister had flown to Moscow and secured Soviet support for the view that neither community in Cyprus should dominate the other. A cultural pact was also signed.

This tentative rapprochement with Russia did not necessarily mean that Turkey was about to abandon its ties to the West. Yet, as one of America's closest students of the country, Richard D. Robinson, has remarked: "Turkish foreign policy may change abruptly without warning or apparent reason." The general alignment with the West was likely to endure, but it could not be predicted that the alliance would be eternal. Those who advocated closer relations with Russia or at least a neutralist position argued that the savings produced by a reduction of the Turkish military establishment would make all the difference in economic development. It could also be argued that economic improvement would in the long run further the democratic cause, since the continuation of economic backwardness is likely to further the growth of extremist feelings.

IN a climate of uncertainty, there are, however, things that are constant, just as the stark geography of Turkey will not change, nor its strategic position. The Turks have a deep attachment to their own heritage, and to those who share it: the passion over Cyprus proves this, if nothing else. The Turks have also surmounted trials that would have caused a weaker people to disintegrate. In the future, as in the past, they will act in their own interest. U.S. support after World War II was of evident value to Turkey. If the Turks continue to receive support and understanding from the West, there is no particular reason why they should change their alignment. But if they come to believe that the Western alliance exists only for the benefit of the West, then the chances are that they will play a more independent role with the same courage and energy that they have displayed on other occasions for other causes.

The other certainty goes deeper than any question of political alliance. A Turkish proverb says: "The arrow has left the bow." The reader of Turkish history sees what powerful trajectories the Turkish arrow took when released from the bow of Islam, how in two centuries this sober, courageous people created a great new empire straddling Europe, Asia and Africa. It is likely that the Turkish arrow will continue to fly on an equally powerful new trajectory now that it has been released by a secular revolution and launched toward a more prosaic but perhaps more important target—the gaining of a better life for the people of Anatolia.

Amid the fallen columns of an ancient Roman bath, vacationers disport themselves in the warm springs of a hotel pool at Pamukkale.

TRADITIONS OF GREATNESS *and national pride sustain Turkey's people . . .*

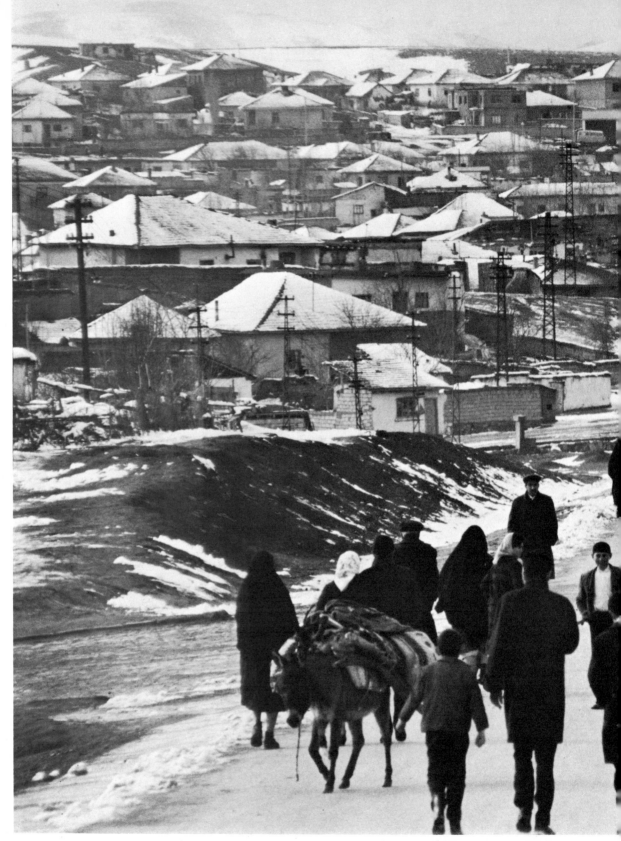

Pedestrians and heavily burdened donkeys travel along a hilly road through a modern village, one of a number that have sprung

. . . as they wrestle with profound problems of technological backwardness an

150

round Ankara. Motorized transport is rarely seen even on this road, which is the principal route from the nation's capital to the east.

illage isolation in an effort to transform their ancient homeland into a modern nation

Appendix

HISTORICAL DATES

B.C.	
2000-1200	A people known as the Hittites establish control over the central Anatolian plateau
c.1200	Peoples from the Aegean migrate into Anatolia. The Hittite kingdom crumbles
c.1200-700	Phrygians dominate the interior of Anatolia
687-546	After developing a civilization in western Anatolia, the kingdom of Lydia is conquered by Cyrus of Persia
334	Alexander the Great establishes control over Anatolia
323	Alexander's empire is divided among his generals. The Romans make inroads in Anatolia, and control all of it by the end of the First Century A.D.
A.D.	
330	Constantine I shifts his capital from Rome to Constantinople, which will become the center of the Byzantine Empire
11th Century	Seljuk Turks move westward into Anatolia
1071	In the Battle of Manzikert the Seljuk Turks defeat the Byzantine Army
1290-1326	Osman I, a Turkish tribal leader, expands his territory near Nicaea at the expense of the disintegrating Byzantine Empire. He becomes the eponymous founder of the Osmanlı, or Ottoman, state and dynasty
1361	Crossing into Europe, the Ottomans capture Adrianople and make it their capital. A corps of Janissaries, or "new troops," recruited from conquered peoples, is organized
1453	Mehmet II, "The Conqueror," takes Constantinople, an event that marks the demise of the Byzantine Empire
1453-1520	Period of conquest. The Ottoman Empire continues to expand westward, reaching into Albania and to Hungary
1520-1566	During the reign of Süleyman the Magnificent the empire continues to expand. At his death it includes not only Anatolia but most of Hungary, the Balkans, the Middle East, the northern coast of Africa and territory along the Red Sea and the Persian Gulf
1574	Under the ineffectual Murad III the Ottoman Empire begins a general deterioration
1683	Ottoman forces fail to take Vienna in a final assault
1699	Under the Treaty of Karlowitz the Turks cede Hungary to Austria and other territories to Venice and Poland
1768-1774	War between Turkey and Russia. The Turks lose the Crimea and Russia obtains navigational rights in Turkish waters and the right to "protect" Orthodox Christian subjects in the Ottoman Empire
1821-1830	Aided by France, Russia and Britain, the Greeks win independence from the Ottomans
1826	Sultan Mahmud II abolishes the Janissary corps
1839	Sultan Abdul Mejid proclaims the equality of all Ottoman subjects
1853-1856	The Crimean War between Russia and the Ottoman Empire, France and Britain. Turkey regains the Crimea and Russia relinquishes its claims of protection over Turkish Christians
1876	Midhat Pasha, dominant reformer of the 19th Century, leads in the deposition of Sultan Abdül Aziz. The first Turkish Constitution is proclaimed
1877	Opening of the first Turkish parliament. Sultan Abdül Hamid soon dissolves it and abrogates the 1876 Constitution
1878	In return for British support in a territorial quarrel with Russia, the Ottomans permit the British to occupy Cyprus
1908	Young Turk revolution restores the Constitution of 1876
1909	Sultan Abdül Hamid is deposed
1912-1913	Turkey loses most of its European territory during the Balkan Wars
1914	The Turks enter World War I on the side of the Central Powers
1915	The Turks successfully defend the Dardanelles against Allied attack, an operation in which Mustafa Kemal (Atatürk) distinguishes himself
1916-1918	Britain takes Ottoman provinces in the Middle East. Allied forces occupy Constantinople and parts of Anatolia
1919	Greek forces invade at Smyrna. Turkish nationalists led by Mustafa Kemal determine to resist the Allies and prevent the dismemberment of Turkey
1920	The nationalists form a provisional Government at Ankara headed by Mustafa Kemal. Greeks advance deeper into Anatolia. The Sultan's Government signs Treaty of Sèvres, which would have virtually dissolved the Ottoman Empire and broken up the Turkish homeland
1922	The nationalists rout the Greek Army and take Smyrna. The Allies negotiate peace with the nationalist Government. The sultanate is abolished
1923	The Treaty of Lausanne concludes peace between Allies and the Turks. The Republic of Turkey is proclaimed with Mustafa Kemal as President. Ankara becomes the capital
1923-1938	Period of great revolutionary reform and "Westernization" under Mustafa Kemal Atatürk. Islam is abolished as the state religion
1945	After remaining neutral during most of World War II, Turkey declares war on Germany and Japan. Turkey becomes a charter member of the U.N.
1947	The U.S. begins its assistance program to Turkey
1950-1952	Turkey joins NATO and supports the U.N. effort in Korea
1950	The opposition Democrat Party wins first free, two-party election in Turkish history. Celâl Bayar becomes President and Adnan Menderes Premier
1955	Violence breaks out between Turkish and Greek communities on the island of Cyprus
1960	Cyprus gains independence from Britain. An Army junta under General Cemal Gürsel takes power in Turkey. Several members of the Democrat Government, including Premier Adnan Menderes, are tried and later executed
1961	Martial law ends. Elections are held. Gürsel is elected President and Ismet Inönü becomes Premier
1964	Turkey is elected an associate member of the European Common Market and launches a long-term development plan
1964	After an outbreak of violence between Turkish and Greek Cypriots, U.N. forces move into Cyprus to keep the peace. The trouble on the island strains relations between Greece and Turkey

152

FOR FURTHER READING

CHAPTER 1: LAND AND PEOPLE

Cuddon, J. A., *The Owl's Watchsong; A Study of Istanbul*. Horizon Press, 1962.

Falk, André, *Turkey*. The Viking Press, 1963.

Kinross, Lord, *Turkey*. The Viking Press, 1959. *Within the Taurus*. William Morrow and Company, 1955.

Riza, Ali, *The Land and People of Turkey*. The Macmillan Company, 1958.

Yalman, Ahmed Emin, *Turkey in My Time*. University of Oklahoma Press, 1956.

CHAPTER 2: EARLY CONQUERORS

Attwater, Donald, *The Christian Churches of the East*, Vol. II. The Bruce Publishing Company, 1947.

Ceram, G. W., *The Secret of the Hittites*. Alfred A. Knopf, 1956.

Gurney, O. R., *The Hittites*. Penguin Books, 1952.

Hitti, Philip K., *The Near East in History; A 5,000 Year Story*. D. Van Nostrand Company, Inc., 1961.

Lloyd, Seton, *Early Anatolia*. Penguin Books, 1956.

Muller, Herbert J., *The Loom of History*. Harper & Brothers, 1958.

Seymour, Thomas Day, *Life in the Homeric Age*. The Macmillan Company, London, 1914.

Zernov, Nicolas, *Eastern Christendom*. G. P. Putnam's Sons, 1961.

CHAPTERS 3 AND 4: SELJUKS AND OTTOMANS

Barthold, W., *Turkestan Down to the Mongol Invasion*. Oxford University Press, 1928.

Creasy, Edward S., *History of the Ottoman Turks*. Khayats, Beirut, 1961.

Czaplicka, M. A., *The Turks of Central Asia in History and at the Present Day*. Clarendon Press, Oxford, 1918.

Edib, Halide, *The Turkish Ordeal*. Century, 1928. *Turkey Faces West*. Yale University Press, 1930.

Eversley, Lord, and Sir Valentine Chirol, *The Turkish Empire*. T. Fisher Unwin Ltd., London, 1924.

Hasluck, F. W., *Christianity and Islam under the Sultans*. Clarendon Press, Oxford, 1929.

Hitti, Philip K., *History of the Arabs*. St. Martin's Press, Inc., 1961.

Lewis, Bernard, *Istanbul and the Civilization of the Ottoman Empire*. University of Oklahoma Press, 1963.

Lewis, Geoffrey, *Turkey*. Frederick A. Praeger, 1965.

Lybyer, Albert Howe, *The Government of the Ottoman Empire in the Time of Suleiman the Magnificent*. Harvard University Press, 1913.

Mardin, Serif, *The Genesis of Young Ottoman Thought*. Princeton University Press, 1962.

Marriott, Sir John Arthur Ransome, *The Eastern Question*. Clarendon Press, Oxford, 1940.

Price, M. Philips, *A History of Turkey from Empire to Republic*. George Allen & Unwin Ltd., London, 1956.

Ramsaur, Ernest Edmondson Jr., *The Young Turks*. Princeton University Press, 1957.

Rice, Tamara Talbot, *The Seljuks*. Frederick A. Praeger, 1961.

Wittek, Paul, *The Rise of the Ottoman Empire*. Luzac and Co. Ltd., 1958.

Yale, William, *The Near East; A Modern History*. The University of Michigan Press, 1958.

Yalman, Ahmed Emin, *Turkey in the World War*. Yale University Press, 1930.

CHAPTERS 5 AND 7: ATATÜRK AND AFTERMATH

Allen, Henry E., *The Turkish Transformation*. University of Chicago Press, 1935.

Economic Mission to Turkey, *The Economy of Turkey*. International Bank for Reconstruction and Development, 1951.

Frey, Frederick W., *The Turkish Political Elite*. The M.I.T. Press, 1965.

Karpat, Kemal H., *Turkey's Politics; The Transition to a Multi-Party System*. Princeton University Press, 1959.

Kinross, Lord, *Atatürk*. William Morrow and Company, 1965.

Lewis, Bernard, *The Emergence of Modern Turkey*. Oxford University Press, 1961.

Robinson, Richard D., *The First Turkish Republic*. Harvard University Press, 1963.

Rustow, Dankwart A., "The Army and the Founding of the Turkish Republic." *World Politics*, XI (July 1959).

Thomas, Lewis V., and Richard N. Frye, *The United States and Turkey and Iran*. Harvard University Press, 1951.

Ward, Robert E., and Dankwart A. Rustow, eds., *Political Modernization in Japan and Turkey*. Princeton University Press, 1964.

Webster, Donald Everett, *The Turkey of Atatürk*. The American Academy of Political and Social Science, 1939.

CHAPTER 6: THE ANATOLIAN HOMELAND

Kemal, Yashar, *Memed, My Hawk*. Pantheon Books, 1961.

Kolars, John F., *Tradition, Season, and Change in a Turkish Village*. NAS-NRC Foreign Field Research Program Report No. 15, University of Chicago, 1963.

Makal, Mahmout, *A Village in Anatolia*. Vallentine, Mitchell, London, 1954.

Stirling, Paul, *Turkish Village*. Weidenfeld and Nicolson, 1965.

CHAPTER 8: THE ARTS

And, Metin, *A History of Theatre and Popular Entertainment in Turkey*. Forum, Ankara, 1963-1964.

Eren, Nuri, *Turkey Today—And Tomorrow*. Frederick A. Praeger, 1963.

Gibb, E. J., *A History of Ottoman Poetry*. Luzac and Co., London, 1905.

Karpat, Kemal H., "Social Themes in Contemporary Turkish Literature." *Middle East Journal* (Winter and Spring, 1960).

Modern Turkish Literature. Turkish Information Office, 1956.

Oz, Tahsin, *Turkish Ceramics*. Turkish Press, Broadcasting and Tourist Department, 1953.

Siyavusgil, Sabri Esat, *Karagoz*. Istanbul, 1961.

Unsal, Behçet, *Turkish Islamic Architecture in Seljuk and Ottoman Times*. Portland Press Ltd., 1959.

Young, T. Cuyler, ed., *Near Eastern Culture and Society*. Princeton University Press, 1951.

CHAPTER 9: SCHISM IN THE SOUL

Frye, Richard N., ed., *Islam and the West*. Mouton & Co., The Hague, 1957.

Marmorstein, Emile, "Religious Opposition to Nationalism in the Middle East." *International Affairs* (July 1952).

Nicholson, Reynold A., *The Mystics of Islam*. Routledge and Kegan Paul Ltd., 1963. *Rumi, Poet and Mystic*. George Allen & Unwin Ltd., 1950.

Phelan, Nancy, *Welcome the Wayfarer*. St. Martin's Press, 1965.

Reed, Howard A., "Revival of Islam in Secular Turkey." *Middle East Journal* (Summer 1954).

CHAPTER 10: THE FUTURE

Eren, Nuri, *Turkey Today—And Tomorrow*. Frederick A. Praeger, 1963.

Kilic, Altemur, *Turkey and the World*. Public Affairs Press, 1959.

Lewis, Geoffrey, *Turkey*. Frederick A. Praeger, 1965.

Rustow, Dankwart A., "Turkey's Second Try at Democracy." *The Yale Review* (Summer 1963).

Weiker, Walter F., *The Turkish Revolution 1960-1961*. The Brookings Institution, 1963.

FAMOUS TURKISH CULTURAL FIGURES AND THEIR PRINCIPAL WORKS

Yusuf Has Hacib	11th Century	Poet; author of *Kutadgu Bilig*, a massive philosophical treatise in verse on government, justice and ethics
Kaşgarlı Mahmut	11th Century	Philologist; compiler of *Divan ü Lûgat-it Türk*, a Turkish grammar and anthology of Turkish literature
Mevlâna Celaleddin Rumi	1207-1273	Mystic poet and philosopher; wrote a six-volume Persian *Mesnevî* of nearly 26,000 couplets on mysticism and morality
Yunus Emre	1238-c.1320	Mystic poet who wrote in the folk tradition and in the classical vein
Süleyman Celebi	?-1422	Religious poet; *Mevlid-i Serif*, a panegyric for Mohammed which is chanted as a requiem
Ali Sir Nevai	1441-1501	Poet and littérateur; *Divans*, or collections of poems, *Muhakemet-ül Lugateyn, Hamse*
Fuzuli	c.1495-1556	Greatest figure of Turkish classical poetry; *Divans* in Turkish, Persian, and Arabic; *Leyla vü Mecnun*, long verse narrative of mystic love
Pir Sultan Abdal	16th Century	Mystic-lyric folk poet
Baki	1526-c.1599	Poet; *Divan*
Nef'i	1582-1635	Poet and satirist; *Divan, Siham-ı Kaza*
Karacaoğlan	c.1606-c.1680	Folk poet who wrote of love and pastoral beauty
Kâtip Celebi	1609-1657	Historian, geographer, travel writer; *Cihan-nüma, Fezleke, Keşf-üz-Zünun*
Evliya Celebi	1611-1682	Author of a 10-volume travel book: *Seyahatname*
Naima	1655-1716	Historian; *Naima Tarihi*
Nedim	?-1730	Poet of love and life in Istanbul; *Divan*
Seyh Galip	1757-1799	Poet; *Divan; Hüsn ü Aşk*, verse allegory of passionate mysticism
Cevdet Paşa	1822-1895	Historian and grammarian; *Tarih-i Cevdet*
Ziya Paşa	1825-1870	Poet and publicist, exponent of social and political reforms; *Terkib-i Bend, Terci-i Bend*
Şinasi	1826-1871	Playwright, poet, journalist, translator; introduced European modes; *Sair Evlenmesi, Müntehabat-ı Eş'ar*
Namık Kemal	1840-1888	Poet, playwright, journalist, novelist; *Vatan Yahut Silistre, Intibah*
Eşref	1846-1912	Poet and satirist; *Deccal, Sah ve Padişah*
Recaizade Ekrem	1847-1914	Poet, playwright, novelist and critic; *Araba Sevdası, Talim-i Edebiyat, Zemzeme*
Abdülhak Hamit Tarhan	1852-1937	Poet and playwright; *Makber, Finten*
Hüseyin Rahmi Gürpınar	1864-1944	Novelist; *Sıpsevdi, Gulyabani*
Ahmet Rasim	1864-1932	Essayist and short-story writer
Halit Ziya Uşaklıgil	1866-1945	Novelist; *Mai ve Siyah, Aşk-ı Memnu*
Tevfik Fikret	1867-1915	Lyric and patriotic poet; *Rübab-ı Sikeste*
Mehmet Akif Ersoy	1873-1936	Religious and patriotic poet; *Safahat*
Ziya Gökalp	1875-1924	Poet and social philosopher whose writings influenced Atatürk; *Kızıl Elma, Türkçülüğün Esasları*
Omer Seyfettin	1884-1920	Short-story writer, social commentator and satirist; *Bomba, Efruz Bey, Yüksek Okçeler*
Ahmet Haşim	1884-1933	Poet and essayist; major Turkish symbolist
Yahya Kemal Beyatlı	1884-1958	Neo-classical poet who wrote of love and of Istanbul's history and beauty
Halide Edib	1884-1964	Major woman novelist; *The Clown and his Daughter, The Turkish Ordeal*
Reşat Nuri Güntekin	1886-1956	Author of popular novels, playwright and short-story writer; *The Autobiography of a Turkish Girl; Afternoon Sun*
Yakup Kadri Karaosmanoğlu	1889-	Novelist and short-story writer; *Kiralık Konak, Nur Baba, Yaban, Panorama*
Fuat Köprülü	1890-	Literary historian; *Türk Dili ve Edebiyatı Hakkında Arastırmalar, Türk Edebiyatı Tarihi*
Nurullah Ataç	1898-1957	Influential critic; *Günlerin Getirdiği, Ararken, Prospero ile Caliban*
Nazım Hikmet Ran	1902-1963	Poet and playwright; *Seyh Bedrettin Destanı, Taranta Babu'ya Mektuplar, Kurtuluş Savaşı Destanı*
Necip Fazıl Kısakürek	1905-	Poet, playwright and essayist; *Ben ve Otesi, Cile, Bir Adam Yaratmak*
Sait Faik Abasıyanık	1906-1954	Short-story writer and novelist; *Semaver, Lüzumsuz Adam, Kumpanya, Alemdağda Var Bir Yılan*
Sabahattin Ali	1907-1948	Novelist and short-story writer; *Kuyucaklı Yusuf, İçimizdeki Seytan, Yeni Dünya, Sırça Köşk*
Sabahattin Eyüboğlu	1908-	Literary critic, translator and essayist
Cahit Sıtkı Tarancı	1911-1956	Poet; *Otuz Beş Yaş*
Orhan Veli Kanık	1914-1950	Poet and translator, depicted everyday life in free verse, using colloquial idioms; *Bütün Siirleri*
Oktay Rifat	1914-	Poet, playwright and translator; *Yaşayip Olmek, Aşk ve Avarelik Ustüne, Siirler, Ikilik*
Orhan Kemal	1914-	Novelist and short-story writer; *Ekmek Kavgası, Murtaza, Kanlı Topraklar*
Fazıl Hüsnü Dağlarca	1914-	Turkey's greatest living poet; *Cocuk ve Allah, Uç Sehitler Destanı, Asu, Aç Yazı*
Aziz Nesin	1915-	Humorist who wrote short stories, plays, poems and novels; *Damda Deli Var, Biraz Gelir misiniz, Zübük-Kağnı Gölgesindeki It*
Melih Cevdet Anday	1915-	Poet, translator and essayist; *Telgrafhane, Kolları Bağlı Odiseus*
Behçet Necatigil	1915-	Poet and translator; *Çevre, Dar Çağ, Yaz Dönemi*
Yaşar Kemal	1922-	Novelist, short-story writer and essayist; *Memed, My Hawk; Ortadirek, Wind from the Plains*
Mahmut Makal	1933-	Author of an important book on village life; *A Village in Anatolia*

ART AND ARCHITECTURE

Seyh Hamdullah	early 16th Century	Master of Islamic-Turkish calligraphy
Hayreddin	early 16th Century	Major architect; Beyazıt II Mosque
Sinan	c.1489-c.1578	Greatest Turkish architect: more than 340 buildings including Süleymaniye, Selimiye, Valde Sultan Mosques

Nigari	1494-1574	Miniaturist
Davud Ağa	?-1595	Architect; Incili Köşk, Murad III Mausoleum
Dalgıç Ahmet Çavuş	?-1605	Architect; Yeni Cami (New Mosque)
Abdullah Buhari	18th Century	Miniaturist
Levnî	?-1732	Greatest master of Turkish miniature art
Ibrahim Callı	1882-1960	Landscapes and portraits
Hikmet Onat	1884-	Still lifes and portraits
Feyhaman Duran	1888-	Landscapes, portraits, still lifes
Cemal Tollu	1899-	Landscapes and still lifes
Zeki Kocamemi	1900-	Early modernizer of Turkish painting
Fahrünnisa Zeid	c.1904-	Leading abstract painter
Nurullah Berk	1906-	Pioneer of modernism in Turkish painting
Zühtü Müridoğlu	1906-	Leading sculptor
Abidin Dino	1911-	Foremost exponent of realism
Bedri Rahmi Eyüboğlu	1913-	Versatile painter who depicts the Turkish scene and uses folk themes
Eren Eyüboğlu	1913-	French-born Turkish nonfigurative painter
Nuri Iyem	1915-	Nonfigurative painter
Ilhan Koman	1921-	Abstract sculptor
Nejad Devrim	1923-	Abstract painter

MUSIC

Hafız Post	?-c.1690	Prolific composer of secular and religious music
Mustafa Itrî	?-c.1712	Greatest figure of Turkish classical music
Hamamizade Ismail Dede	1777-1845	A master of religious music and secular songs
Sakir Ağa	19th Century	Songs and instrumental music
Hacı Arif Bey	1831-1884	Popular romantic songs
Lem'i Atlı	1869-1945	Popular lyric songs and instrumental music
Cemal Reşit Rey	1905-	Operatic and symphonic music, operettas and concertos, chamber music, piano selections
Ulvi Cemal Erkin	1906-	Symphony, concertos, incidental music
Ahmet Adnan Saygun	1907-	*Yunus Emre Oratorio;* operatic and orchestral works
Bülent Arel	1918-	Composer of electronic music
Ilhan Usmanbaş	1921-	Symphonic and chamber music
Nevit Kodallı	1924-	*Atatürk* Oratorio, *Van Gogh* Opera

Credits

The sources for the illustrations in this book appear below. Credits for pictures from left to right are separated by commas, from top to bottom by dashes.

Cover—Farrell Grehan
8—Farrell Grehan
13—Map by Rafael Palacios
15 through 24—Farrell Grehan
26—Map by Rafael Palacios
31, 32—Ara Güler
33 through 38—Farrell Grehan
41—Map by Rafael Palacios
46 through 51—Farrell Grehan
52, 53—Left; Farrell Grehan; right; Henri Cartier-Bresson from Magnum
54, 55—The Radio Times Hulton Picture Library
59—Culver Pictures
61 through 70—Farrell Grehan
78, 79—Ara Güler; except bottom right Julien Bryan
80 through 85—Farrell Grehan

90—*The Koran Interpreted*, 1955, by Arthur J. Arberry, The Macmillan Company
92 through 97—Farrell Grehan
98, 99—Farrell Grehan except bottom left; Ara Güler
100, 101—Farrell Grehan
102—Ara Güler
107—Center and right drawings reproduced with the permission of Charles Scribner's Sons from *The Mode in Hats and Headdress* pp. 35, 37 by R. Turner Wilcox copyright 1945 (c) 1959
110, 111—Mehmet Surenkok, Ara Güler—Ara Güler, United Press International

112—James Burke
113—Ara Güler
114, 115—Brian Seed
116, 117—Farrell Grehan
120—*Karagoz* by Sabri Esat Siyavusgil, The Turkish Press, Broadcasting and Tourist Department
123 through 127—Farrell Grehan
128—James Whitmore
129—Farrell Grehan
130—Left; Farrell Grehan—Ara Güler (2) right; Farrell Grehan
131—Farrell Grehan
132, 133—Ara Güler
138—Farrell Grehan
139, 140—Ara Güler
141 through 144—Farrell Grehan
149, 150, 151—Farrell Grehan

ACKNOWLEDGMENTS

The editors are indebted to Kemal H. Karpat, Associate Professor of Comparative Government and International Relations, New York University Graduate School of Arts and Science; and to Geoffrey Lewis, Fellow of St. Antony's College and Senior Lecturer in Turkish, the University of Oxford. Both read and commented on the entire text. Valuable help was also provided by Talat Sait Halman, Turkish critic and translator. The author wishes to express his appreciation to Michael Austin, Instructor in Humanities, Robert College, Istanbul.

Index

This symbol in front of a page number indicates a photograph or painting of the subject mentioned.

Production staff for Time Incorporated
John L. Hallenbeck (Vice President and Director of Production)
Robert E. Foy, Caroline Ferri and Robert E. Fraser
Text photocomposed under the direction of
Albert J. Dunn and Arthur J. Dunn

x

Printed by R. R. Donnelley & Sons Company, Crawfordsville, Indiana
and The Safran Printing Company, Detroit, Michigan
Bound by R. R. Donnelley & Sons Company, Crawfordsville, Indiana
Paper by The Mead Corporation, Dayton, Ohio
Cover stock by The Plastic Coating Corporation, Holyoke, Massachusetts

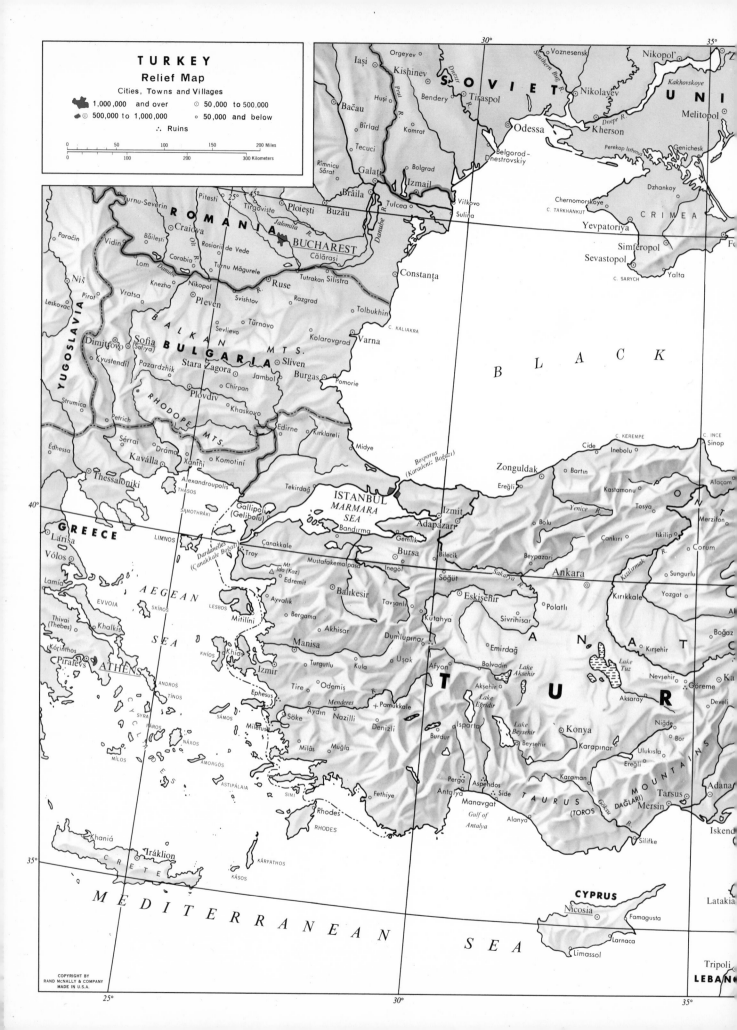